REACH YOUR GOALS

ANGELA MOFFAT

Dedication

FOR DOROTHY AND PETER MOFFAT

'SPERO MELIORA'

[I aspire to greater things]

CONTENTS

Introduction

I decided to write this book because writing a book is one of the main things that is on my bucket list, and I wanted to pass on the various things that I have learned on the path to achieving my own goals, step-by-step.

I believe that all of us can change our lives for the better and can also get more of what we want – we can all achieve our goals and can do so more easily with the guidance of this book. Maybe your goals include things like getting a certain job; starting your own business; being good at sports; or even traveling around the world. Whatever it is that you want most of in life, my aim is to help you achieve your goals – or at least some of them – more easily!

By following a few simple rules and learning about the different techniques that you can apply to everyday life, you can find that it helps you to build a strong foundation from where you will likely find that things begin to flow into your life faster, more easily, and better than they did before.

Look at this foundation as a springboard to success. Of course, you must be willing to put in the work and effort required to reach any goals, but by using this method it should become easier for you to achieve those goals and also help you to focus on what it is that needs to be done. Start from scratch and working your way up step-by-step, stage by stage, until you have achieved the goals you want in life by using the simple method contained in this book. All successful people have a plan, and if you also wish to be successful then you must have a plan as well.

I left school at 16 with no plan and I'm sure that not many people would have thought that I would make a successful life for myself. It has taken many years of mixed results to finally find a method that worked, so that I could reach my goals. I wish I had known back then what I now know; my journey would have been a lot easier. It was a hard journey, and it need not have been. Had I known at the time, all those years ago, what I now know then reaching my goals would have been a lot easier and also a lot faster.

One day I realised how I could get more of what I wanted and how I could successfully reach my goals. It worked! I could not believe that it was such a simple technique that everyone can try.

Today I am a clinical hypnotherapist and a holistic therapist; I use my skills to help people become their better selves, and I have also worked in the charity sector for many years.

I have written this book for everyone out there who wants to get better results in achieving their goals, overcoming any blocks and obstacles that are in the way, and for those who want to create better lives for themselves.

I hope you enjoy reading this book and that you achieve the things that you want for yourself.

So, are you ready to learn about how I reached my goals and how a tiny percentage of the population are also using this method to reach their goals as well? Good, then let's take that first step and begin the journey to finding your success.

CHAPTER 1
What do you want?

I believe that each person has the ability for greatness, something they were born to do. Each of us has this inbuilt ability to achieve our dreams and our goals in life and become the person we want to be. This may seem like a pretty big statement to make, but human beings are capable of doing so much more than they think they can. However, many people put limits on themselves throughout their life and do not think they can do much to reach any goals that they may have, as they always seem to be out of reach, too hard to achieve, and a lot of us are just not sure how or where to begin.

It is also true that many people are not sure exactly what it is they want to achieve. Perhaps they have had some ideas but have not been able to decide on a specific goal. They may have thought about it for a while, then given up; or perhaps they did know what they wanted to achieve and have tried different ways of reaching their goal or dream and they have failed each time. After the first or second failure, maybe it became easier to move on to something else, something less frustrating, something that was less daunting, or even to give up altogether. No doubt this would leave a person feeling saddened and despondent that they could not reach that goal; they tried but it just did not work out. This can often happen to people; they have not put something in place to make reaching their goals a little easier. Don't beat yourself up about it, if this has applied to you, there is a simple method to help you reach goals, a simple system to try. You must find out exactly what you want – I mean what you really want! This is very important as it would be difficult to begin anything without first knowing this.

So, first you must know what it is you want to do. This sounds obvious, but so many people don't really know, or perhaps they only think they know, what it is they want from life. Work for instance, many people just drift into an area of work, they are good at it and it pays the bills, so they do not question it and carry on doing that job. If people are happy with that, then fine, but what if there is something more that they want, something they've dreamt of for a long time and it did not occur to them to even try to attempt it or at least give it a go?

This could be because of a fear of failure, or maybe it is a lack of knowledge or contacts that may be holding them back from attempting their goals. So, how do you go about setting your goals and achieving **your** dream? As I have already said, you need to find out exactly what you want, what it is you **really** want to do in life. Do your abilities and present mindset make it possible? Are you prepared to put in the effort required?

Firstly, to help you find out what you really want to do and a possible course of action, sit down and make a list of all your personal likes and dislikes; then ask yourself what talents you have, what qualifications do you have and what are your ambitions and goals. You should write it on A4 paper and include all the things that you need to ask yourself, plus you will also need to write down answers to some of the following questions and anything else that comes to mind that is relevant to your personal circumstances.

- What do I like doing in my spare time?
- What am I good at?

- How much money do I have to put towards my goals?
- Have I analysed my appearance and habits?
- Do I work better on my own or with other people?
- How much free time do I have each day, or weekend, to progress towards my goal?
- When, or if, I daydream, what was I daydreaming I was doing?
- Do I have any bad or unhealthy habits to overcome?
- Using a scale of 1 – 10, 10 being the highest, how determined am I to achieve goals and improve my life?
- What kind of goals am I interested in achieving?
- Am I happy in my work?
- What kind of career or hobby do I wish I had?
- Will my family and friends be supportive?
- Will I need training, support or a mentor?
- How healthy am I at the moment?

These are the main questions that you will need to ask yourself. You should see a pattern begin to emerge. Of course, add anything that you need to, after all it is your list. Add your answers under each question and be as detailed as possible, and also be as honest with yourself as you can be. Examine what you have written, does it help you decide a course of action? Add things to the list whenever something new occurs to you as well. The answers you have given will give you clues as to a possible career choice, or the type of work that you should be aiming for, as well as what to avoid, what needs to change, what type of hobby or dream goal you should aim for, and what resources you currently have available to you. Everyone should know what they want to do in life, otherwise you can't even begin making progress towards any goals that you may have. Unless you can figure out exactly what you want then you cannot plan the way forward. Always know, always have a plan for your life, and always have goals. I will say it again in big huge letters. Copy it out and pin it to your fridge if you want, as long as you see it and read it every day, it **really** is that important!

ALWAYS HAVE A PLAN FOR YOUR LIFE AND ALWAYS HAVE GOALS.

So, what you have written down is your personal list for looking at different areas of your life; what kind of person you are; what might suit you best, and how you are currently situated in your life. It should become obvious when you have finished writing it as to what it is that needs to change or improve and hopefully what kind of goals you are interested in.

You can now make a goals list; for example, if you have written that you want to start a business, add the type of business and its name. Of course, your goal can be anything but make sure to list it, describe how you see it working out, and how you see it being a success. Also, give it a time frame, depending on what it is. For example, lose weight over the next 6 – 9 months. Give yourself a deadline and aim to complete certain goals and dreams by that date, if it's possible. This will give you a push and prompt you to take the actions that are required in a more determined and focused way which will usually lead to a more successful outcome.

Time frames can change, of course, life happens and there may be delays! So, things may sometimes take longer to complete, but as long as it is not put off for too long it should be okay. Don't leave things for weeks or even months! As that can lead to you losing focus, and it's important to really focus on any steps that you will need to take on a daily or weekly basis. Write it down, and then make it happen. So few people do this, but it really does make a difference. Try it and see for yourself. The physical act of writing the steps and your goals down means that it's there in front of you and it becomes something real, rather than just an idea you have in your head, and when something's real, it becomes hard to ignore that it isn't. Hopefully this book will help you discover what it is you want to do in life; what you are meant to do in life; and help you to be able to go out into the world and achieve whatever that may be. When you know what you want you can then begin to plan towards that goal. I once knew a gentleman who didn't really know what he wanted out of life, and he floated from job to job, and from town to town, in search of something that would make him happy. Every now and then he would get the urge to move to a new house because he was convinced it would be better elsewhere; somehow, life would be better someplace else. So, he spent his whole life looking for this mythical place where everything would just fall into place and feel right – he would then be happy and find contentment. That was his goal. It didn't happen because there was no such place. What he didn't understand was that the thing he was looking for was inside himself, the answers lay within him, and he just never understood that. He didn't realise that what he should have been wanting from life was to be content with himself, to make friends with himself, to gain confidence and make peace with certain aspects of his own past. A rather unhappy past. If he had realised that was what he should have wanted for himself then his whole life would have been very different, and he would have eventually found that contentment. When you're deciding what it is you want, look inside yourself first to make sure that what you want exists, and is the right thing to do for yourself and your family, and for your long-term happiness and contentment. If it does exist, then give yourself the green light and go for it! Therefore, we can ascertain that you must know exactly what you want, that is what's vital, that's a given. Not being sure what you're aiming for means you can't begin taking any steps towards any goal. Be clear in your aims and the direction that you want to go in. If you have several goals and can't decide which one to go for first, then start with the smallest one and then tackle the bigger ones after you have completed that one. Build up to bigger and better goals. Have faith that you can work out exactly what you want from life, and when you know, you can then begin taking steps and making plans. When deciding what you want, it's also necessary to be selfish, as you can't always be sacrificing your time, your energy, your goals and your dreams for other people. This will wear you down and eventually it will end up making you unhappy, so you must find the right balance so that you can keep others happy, but at the same time, everyone should know when it's your time to do things for yourself. I can't stress enough how important this is. When figuring out a way forward, decide on the things that make you happy, and the things that don't. What's happening in your world that makes you sad, unhappy, drags you down, and depletes your energy? These things need to go or be fixed or rearranged to suit you better. Put these things on your list, and list the steps needed to sort this out. Be happy! Don't put up with being unhappy, because that's a waste of your precious time, time that could be spent doing loads of other more productive, positive, constructive, or life fulfilling activities. Don't hold back from telling the people around you that you want to do things; things that mean you can reach your goals – and have some quality me time while you're doing them as well. Let those closest to you know what you want to do, be precise, don't be vague about it, if you are then they won't think you're being serious and may dismiss your idea altogether, and then you will feel less confident about doing it. Get everything straight in your mind regarding what you need and what you want, then write it all down in your lists under the appropriate heading or question. For example, you may have thought:

My family don't think I can do anything other than be a housekeeper for them. Write this down. You will now need to figure out the steps you need to take in order to change this. So, here you could add the steps underneath this heading that you need to take to sort this out, for example:

- Speak to my husband (or whoever is closest) and tell them I would like to start doing some things for myself and have a bit of extra time for myself.
- Delegate certain tasks.
- Call a family meeting – be positive, keep your voice even, keep the meeting upbeat, but be firm regarding the changes you need. If you're not happy say so.
- Make a start on all your lists, so you know where you're headed.

"Concentrate all of your thoughts upon the work at hand.
The sun's rays do not burn until brought into focus."
– Alexander Graham Bell

CHAPTER 2
Getting Unstuck

It is normal to get stuck – stuck in your habits, stuck in a job, stuck in your environment and stuck in your thinking. STUCK! So, don't beat yourself up about it, just realise that you need to start making some changes in your life, and take actions to do something about it and achieve the results that you need. Making your lists and building them up by adding more information can help. Keep working on them and keep going back to them from time to time, adding more ideas. A pattern should emerge, and a way forward will begin to present itself.

If you still feel a bit stuck after doing your lists and you have run out of ideas or any further information, then you could always keep a dream journal. Why a dream journal? What is that going to achieve, I hear you ask? Well, dreams usually have a meaning behind them; perhaps you've been having the same, or similar, dreams for a long time. Write them down as soon as you wake up in the morning, when they are still clear in your mind. Dreaming is part of the subconscious mind's way of expressing experiences, passions, ideas and deeply held beliefs. What do your dreams tell you about what, or who, you want to be? There may well be a common theme to your dreams. So, why not add your dream information to your list. Analyse your dreams, look inside yourself and you might find the answers to what your inner mind, your subconscious mind, is trying to tell you. Do some research on the meanings of dreams and start keeping that dream journal.

This is only one of the many ways that can help you to decide what it is that you want and also to discover a way that will help you to move forward. So, do not underestimate the power of dreams! Dreams can reveal your true feelings towards something, and sometimes even give you big clues for the future.

If you are stuck because of negative thinking or some unhelpful or bad habits, you could try having hypnotherapy. Hypnosis has a good track record in helping most people with a wide range of issues, including smoking cessation, weight loss, and confidence problems. There is an endless list of issues that can be helped or even eliminated through having hypnosis. Hypnotherapy is very effective at bringing about change in the subconscious mind, which will then begin to be obeyed by the conscious mind. Fact. So, this is definitely something you could consider doing to help you get past any blocks, phobias, or habits that may be holding you back from achieving any number of goals and pushing forward in your life.

Confidence is a major issue that many people have trouble with; it is important for things such as meeting new people and starting a business or getting yourself out there in some way. Some of the richest and most successful people on the planet are those who are the most confident in themselves; the confidence just shines out of them. Other people are naturally drawn to them and admire what they are achieving in their lives. We all want to have that super confident outlook, I'm sure you'll agree.

Maybe what you want is something relatively small like taking a holiday, rather than owning a large business, or running a marathon. Whatever your goal is, following the simple formula within this book should help you to achieve it, or at least I hope that it does! Once you know exactly what you want and what to aim for, it makes the whole journey a lot easier.

Remember, never give up on your dreams, not ever. If people say you'll never do it, if they tear your ideas to shreds, if they laugh at you, just carry on anyway and remember to never give up. The difference between a successful person and a person who gives up too easily is that the successful person is persistent, and has travelled doggedly towards their goals, no matter what. I have faith that you can do this. Never get stuck in a rut, and if that's where you are right now, then never think to yourself that it's a hopeless situation and that you cannot get out of it – there are always ways to change your life for the better. Always. You may not believe this, you may think that there is no way out and that there's nothing to be done about it, that's not true. Even if you start with tiny changes it doesn't matter, a change is a change regardless of how small it may be. So, never think that because you are making small changes or taking small steps that it won't make a difference to you and your goals. It definitely will in the long term, because all of the changes and actions you're taking will start to accumulate over time. On the front cover of this book, you will see the picture of a man – or it could be a woman – climbing up the steps, or ladder, to success and reaching for their goals. That's you, that's what you will be doing once you make a start and realise what you want, and how to untangle yourself from being stuck where you are. Perhaps getting unstuck from something holding you back is your goal, perhaps it is the main thing for you to concentrate on; to overcome and conquer. You can do this by taking one step at a time until you have freed yourself. Don't ever concentrate on the things that you don't want, as this only leads to having more of them, it's a self-fulfilling prophecy. Thinking about the negative will only attract more negativity into your life. That's a fact! This negative thinking becomes your reality, and you create it day by day. Stop! Think in a positive way. Become that person who doesn't settle for second best; the person who can take action and get things sorted out for yourself; who wants better and wants to be unstuck. Here are some of the main things to remember about getting yourself unstuck. Some of which may apply to you and some may not, everyone is different, but have a read through anyhow:

- Recognise any self-doubt and work on that.

- Let go of the past. Write down everything that no longer serves you, and then burn the page, or shred it. Have a little letting go ceremony.

- Change your perspective on what it is that's holding you back, looking at it from another perspective might make it seem easier to overcome.

- Make the small changes first.

- Explore your purpose. Our purpose here on earth should not be just achieving our goals, there's more to life, and your life's purpose, than that. Explore helping others around you, and out in the world, don't forget to help the animals as well, perhaps join a charity and give a donation or sponsor an endangered species. Or maybe even sponsor a child overseas. Your contribution will make a difference.

- Believe in yourself 100%.

- Practice being hopeful every day. Hope levels may deplete a little if you've had a bad day, so it needs topping up regularly. Always have a store of hope.

- Do not let yourself be pessimistic. Pessimism stops progress. Ask yourself why you are feeling this way, what caused it, are you overreacting? Can you do something to improve this? Are you prone to feelings of pessimism? How long have you felt that way?

- What did you like doing as a child?

- What do you enjoy doing now that takes you out of yourself?

- It can be hard to move on after a negative event. Seek help if you need it. People often wait for something outside of themselves to happen to make everything alright. You may wait for a long time! Take action, get it sorted yourself, because what you are looking for is inside you. You alone must make changes, and change needs to happen to get unstuck. Don't be one of the many people walking around who was too scared to make the changes and take the risks; get help, take action, and start to improve those things in life that were causing that miserable mindset and life. Yes, it happens to so many people, that's the sad thing because it could have been very different had they realised how to unstick themselves from a negative pattern. You won't end up that way will you – the answer is NO! Say it out loud – "No I won't get stuck anymore, I will take the actions to sort myself and my future out." Start saying things like this to yourself everyday as you start to prepare to make those changes and begin to realise that your future is there right in front of you, waiting for you to reach for it.

"Every journey starts with a single step."
– Maya Angelou

CHAPTER 3
Steps

Your previous personal lists should be detailing how you see yourself; your likes and dislikes, how you feel about your job, how fit you are and any bad habits that you need to get rid of, and of course all of your goals. These lists will also show you what it is that's possible at the moment as well as what isn't, whilst also showing you what needs to stay in your life and what it is that needs to go. If there is something that needs changing in your life; something that you are not happy with, then put that on the list as one of your goals to sort out as well. Think about all of the steps that are needed to achieve each goal, do some research if necessary, then list all of the actions that will be needed. Each one of these steps must be written in a positive way. For example, if you have written that your main goal is to travel the world and you have listed the places you want to visit in order of preference, then you now need to figure out a way of doing this. Instead of saying: I want to go to Switzerland, but I can't afford it right now and my boss won't give me the time off of work anyway, instead list it in a positive way, list it as the actions that you can take in order to reach that goal. Your list might read like this:

Visit Switzerland (goal):

1. Google Switzerland and find out about the different towns and places to visit.

2. Find out how expensive it is to visit and check the exchange rate.

3. What will it cost me to go there and how long will I want to

stay in Switzerland?

4. Do I have everything that I will need to travel there, for example, clothes, luggage, medication, maps, passports etc.

5. Look into travel insurance and how much it costs.

6. How will I find the money?

7. How long will it take me to save up enough money to fund the trip?

8. Speak to the boss about time off for travel and how much time off I am entitled to.

9. Do I need a new job, or a new boss?

10. Speak to family, what do they think of my plans?

11. Look for jobs in Switzerland, if I'm going solo traveling and want to stay for a period of time; look for working holidays.

12. Do I know someone who has already been there – how did they manage to go, what was their experience of the trip?

Of course, these are just examples of how to break down a goal into the steps that you will need to take to be able to reach that particular goal. The steps may be a lot more, or a lot less, than those that I have described here, as every goal is different and the steps you take will depend on many things that are personal to you. But whatever your goal is in life, be it large or small, you should list each step needed in order to take action and make the necessary changes, and then things will start to happen. Writing down each step makes a plan easier to follow and you will also know exactly what you need to do, and what actions are required. It makes it real.

Ensure that you do your research properly to find out everything that you will need to add to your lists, so that you can take the proper actions required to reach that goal. Make sure that you are not missing anything out, missing information will only hold you up further along the line. When you have listed a particular goal and have listed all the steps needed to help you reach that goal, you will sometimes find that these steps need to then be broken down into even smaller steps, or what I refer to as micro-steps. Relating to the previous example: the goal of traveling to Switzerland, I have listed several steps to take, one of which is to look up working holidays. This could then be broken down into smaller micro-steps. For example, you may want to:

- Look up companies organising working holidays and phone them up to make enquiries about these.

- How much will I need to travel; what insurance do I need; what jobs are available in Switzerland; am I suited to these jobs, and does the company charge me anything for the work placements?

- How long would the job last?

- How much could I earn, and so on and so forth.

These micro-steps are your daily/weekly to-do lists and when they are completed, you can then also tick off that step on your main list.

Perhaps you may even be able to tick off a step each day if it is a straightforward task that you have to do on the list. There will, of course, be much bigger steps on your list, and these will most likely take longer to achieve. Do not worry too much about these, just keep working towards them and finding ways to get what it is you need to be able to complete that step. Even if it takes you a long time, do not give up; keep hacking away at it, piece by piece.

Some years ago, I decided that I wanted to buy a house. I didn't have much money and I needed to have a certain amount to be able to buy something that was half decent. I opened an account just for my savings for the house and spent the next seven years saving every penny I could. This meant that I had to go without holidays, trips out, splashing out on treats etc. It took ages, but I did it and I found a house that I could afford. I now own this house as well as another property. I put this success down to being single-minded and determined to reach my goal of home ownership. I can tell you that I did write many lists during that time to help me to complete each stage that I needed to in order to reach my goal. You can do this too; you just need to be determined and keep your eyes fixed firmly on your dream so that you can make it a reality.

Ticking off the steps on your list is very satisfying, I can tell you. There has been research conducted looking at those who make to-do lists and those who do not; the list-makers were more driven and focused on their goals and achieved far more than the non-list makers. It may seem like a simple way to do things, but it really does work. Try it; when you have ticked off a few steps on your lists, it means you are that much closer to your dream goal. Also remember that if you do fail at something, do not give up; ask yourself why did it fail? What is it I could have done differently? Do your research and find another way to succeed, there is usually a solution out there somewhere, you just need to find it. This of course may mean spending extra time finding the right contacts and information that you may need but have patience and persistence and you will find the answers. Many people give up too soon if they can't find the answers to something straight away. You shouldn't! Experience has taught me that putting in the extra effort really does pay off. Sometimes you might be on the verge of giving up but instead of giving up it is best to take a step back and then revisit it at a later date with fresh eyes, having then given it more thought the solution may well appear to be more obvious. If you fall down ninety-nine times make sure to get back up a hundred times.

"The reward of a thing well done is to of done it."
– Ralph Waldo Emerson

CHAPTER 4
Safety First

Please consider your fitness levels, your medical history and any current health issues you may have when you are making your lists to achieve any goal, especially if your goal involves any physical effort, dieting, taking supplements, or any major changes to your daily routine and any additional stresses that could be involved. Also, carefully consider whether there might be an element of risk-taking involved in some way. If you have any health issues at all, then you must consult your doctor before starting certain projects that could impact your physical or mental health, especially if these projects involve dieting, exercise, or extra stresses. A doctor will be able to tell you if you are physically and psychologically able to proceed with your plans. Also make sure to consult your doctor before taking any supplements.

Supplements

Different types of vitamins, herbs and oils can sometimes interact with certain medications that you may be taking. Various supplements can alter the effectiveness of some medications, so it is a good idea to always check that it is okay and safe by asking your GP/doctor first. You can also check this by consulting with a good health-food shop where they should have a contra-indications book to check if the particular supplement that you want could clash with any medications that you may be taking. If they do not know about what can and cannot be taken safely, then find another shop where they can tell you. Do not just take someone's word for it, do your research. You can of course also take advice from a good herbalist or nutritionist, remember not all supplements are created equal either, so ensure that you are asking the right people for advice.

Risks

Of course, I do not recommend that you take unnecessary risks, that are dangerous, in order to reach your goal. What if you were injured? What if you could not work for a while? What would happen to your family? Perhaps there is something else that you could do that would be less risky? What you are aiming for may not involve any physical risks, but if it does then you should think these through and consider everything carefully first.

Always take advice from the experts who have already done what you are thinking of doing and also those who know all about your current level of fitness. Weigh up the pros and cons. Be careful and be committed to safety, make sure you have the proper equipment and clothes. Also be sure to:

- Set high standards.

- Stay alert.

- Take the lead when it comes to your own safety, and the safety of others.

- Learn how to lift. It may be needed! It's not just down to your strength, there is an actual technique.

- Avoid doing things if you are already fatigued.

- Train to be competent enough to be able to do whatever it is you plan on achieving.

- Do not be a practical joker – it's dangerous, or at least it could be depending on what you happen to be doing.

- Keep all equipment clean and well maintained. Check it often and make sure it meets the necessary regulations.

- Stop when you need to assess the risk.

- If you can't do something, stop and don't try to push yourself beyond your limit. If you need more training, then commit to that so that you can make sure that you are properly prepared and are ready for whatever challenge you are trying to do. Some people prepare for years to reach their challenges and goals, if that's what you need to do then fine, you must be patient and do what you have to do. Don't take short cuts! Especially when it comes to a physical challenge. If you've never exercised before, then I recommend that you start with walking. You could start by doing a ten minute walk each day and build it up slowly from there, and always make sure that you check with a doctor, if you are not used to any exercise, before you begin.

"We have to do the best we can.
This is our sacred human responsibility."
– Albert Einstein

CHAPTER 5

Self-Sabotage – the Subconscious Says No!

The subconscious mind is a bit like a sponge, it soaks up all of our experiences in life and stores them away. If you want to do something and you find that something is blocking you, then it could be your subconscious saying 'no, I don't like that', based on your own previous experiences and negative conditioning. No matter how hard you try with your thinking, conscious mind you just aren't able to do it; you don't feel you could do it, and you also react negatively to it. This kind of reaction to something you really want, or need, to do is usually because of the deeper mind, the subconscious.

For example, perhaps you want to learn to swim. You would like to learn because it looks fun, your friends go swimming, and you want to learn so that you're able to teach your children to swim safely, but because of a negative experience in the past you are terrified and cannot bring yourself to be near water. It is a phobic reaction to a bad experience, and it is just your subconscious mind's way of protecting you. Overcoming things like phobias or blocks such as these can be easy with the use of hypnosis and also by using daily affirmations and taking small practical steps, doing these things can help a person to change a negative into a positive. This is just one example of course. You may want to change any number of things and feel that there is something that is holding you back. Maybe it is a lack of confidence, either to start a business, or you want to train to become fitter and sign up for a gym membership, or anything else that you may be aiming for. Sometimes a lack of confidence will stop you from progressing towards that goal.

Perhaps you have a self-image problem that could be holding

you back. A self-image problem will always hold you back from doing what it is you are dreaming of doing. So, it should be top of any list when looking at what needs to be addressed and sorted out. Hypnosis is also good for this and it's something I can personally recommend. You could also try EFT (Emotional Freedom Techniques) to help with confidence as well.

There are many therapies that can help you with confidence and that have a good success rate, so do not be too shy to try them out. Asking for help if you have something to overcome is necessary, it will be a lot easier if you do ask someone for help, and it will also save you time when you're trying to achieve a goal, and of course you will also feel better about yourself, your situation, your self-image, or whatever else it happens to be. Confidence is a big one to overcome, so be sure to get it sorted if it is something that you struggle with. Not asking for help because you are shy or feel awkward about it will mean things might stay as they are and will not change. You won't want that, I am sure. Be a bit brave and sort out any issues so that you are able to move forward and get a lot more stuff accomplished and achieve a lot more in your life. It is possible. It is, believe me. It will seem difficult at first, that's because if you have low confidence levels, taking action to sort it out will be something that is alien to you. But this is something you must do in order to be in the right mindset to achieve your goals and reach any dreams you have; you have to be confident in yourself and when you are confident you won't be sabotaging yourself anymore.

There are many ways that you might sabotage yourself that will lead to you being unable to obtain your goals. For example, you might turn to food and over-eating, or you might be an undecided person who procrastinates. The sabotage may even be caused by not committing to relationships and choosing to keep people at arm's length because of a deep-seated fear, and not wanting to repeat the past in some way. As we open ourselves up to other people, that in turn means that we are more vulnerable and could experience rejection. If we are rejected, then that further fuels any related insecurities. Perhaps if a person has had an unstable childhood, and has been let down in various ways, then this too will lead to self-sabotaging behaviour. Some of the people who constantly sabotage themselves do so because it makes them feel in control of a situation.

There are ways to help you to stop sabotaging yourself, here are some things that can help:

- Understand any self-destructive behaviours that may have become a habit and get help to eliminate them.

- Recognise the signs of self-sabotage.

- Find out what lies behind any bad habits.

- Find your inner positive voice and mentally overcome the negative choices.

- Do things differently; take action.

- Make lots of small changes and see the positive outcomes from them begin to become larger ones.

- Set your goals, write your lists, always have plans.

- Examine yourself. If you have worked hard towards any of your goals and things still don't work out for you, are you self-sabotaging? Change the approach you use, do things a little differently and see if that works.

- Write down all of your negative beliefs, examine each one. Does a pattern emerge? What lies behind these beliefs? How can you work to change each one, step by step?

- Try some of the techniques and therapies listed in this book.

- Don't give up, human beings are amazing and can overcome many things – including self-sabotage.

- Those who self-sabotage will often experience feelings of worthlessness, and even self-hatred. If this is the case, then you must get it sorted out pronto! If you are feeling like this towards yourself you won't be able to move forward, and if you are reading this and thinking 'yes, that's me', then you will have to sort out these deep seated, underlying beliefs, and begin to have some faith in yourself and your abilities.

Deep down people who self-sabotage do not believe that they

also deserve success! This is very wrong, of course they do, just the same as everyone else does.

Reflect on your behaviour, and what is holding you back, this may take a while to do; sometimes figuring out what is happening in your own mind can take a bit of self-discovery, and that takes time, but it's also necessary to get to the root cause of the issue, so that you can progress. The most successful people are the ones who take the time to think through their decisions, and their actions. Follow their lead and take a page out of their book, so to speak. Then you will be ready to start creating the new you – the goal setting, extraordinary new you, the go getter, the person who you have always known you could be.

"By prevailing over all obstacles and distractions, one may unfailingly arrive at his chosen goal or destination."
– Christopher Columbus

CHAPTER 6

Rewiring the Brain for Success

Most people will agree that you need to be confident if you want to get on well in life, so try having a mental detox and clear out of the rubbish stored in your brain and all those things which have been holding you back. Replace it with new positive learning. Hypnotherapy can help you to do this. Many people were told as a child that they were not good enough in some way, shape or form, perhaps they were even bullied at school to the point where their self-confidence was crushed. Some people will probably bounce back and will not be too bothered, whilst others will suffer for all of their lives from the consequences of being bullied. There are a lot of negative people out there, who delight in dragging others down, because doing so makes them feel better about themselves. It is pretty sad really. Being bullied says more about the person doing the bullying than it does about the person on the receiving end. If you've been told that you're not good enough, or had other similar negative experiences, then you need to realise that it was their issue not yours. If it's affected you, hypnosis is one way that can help you to change any low opinions you may have of yourself, as well as also reading books like this one to help! You don't need to take on other people's negativity and issues, life's too short for all that nonsense; you have better things to do, right? Your time is valuable.

Of course, it may be something completely different that is holding you back from being your better self. This could be due to conditioning. Negative conditioning is probably the main reason why a lot of people do not think they can achieve any goals in life. From the moment we are born, all of our experiences – the environment we grow up in, the people

images, in this case these images will be your goals and any positive outcomes.

Meditation

This is really good; a great deal of research has been done on the effects of meditation on the brain. Meditation can actually change the structure of the brain. Some research even claims that the practice can change our brains in as little as eleven hours. It can help you with so many things including stress and self-awareness, and it is also very likely to lead to more positive emotions.

CBT – Cognitive Behavioural Therapy

This is a talking therapy which aims to change the way you think and behave. It is commonly used for things like anxiety and depression but can also be used for helping with other mental and physical problems. In changing your behaviours, you rewire your brain into healthier patterns.

Remove Yourself from Negative Situations

This is vital. A negative environment is going to drag you down and stop you from progressing. Make a plan to change or escape that situation. It might not be easy, and it may take some time, courage and planning but it will be worth it in the long run. Say, for instance, that you hate your job (and your boss) and have decided that life is too short to put up with all the hassle at work. So, find a new job – not always easy, but add it to your lists as one of your goals and work towards it.

Mindfulness

Mindfulness changes the brain regions and produces changes in the grey matter over time. It helps with things like stress, memory, sense of self etc. This practice concentrates the mind on the present moment through various channels such as meditation.

Find Fresh Ideas

Adding in new, positive ideas and practices actually alters the neurochemistry and structure of the brain. Reading is a good way to help you do this and become better informed, whilst also helping the process of rewiring the brain.

Focus on your Long-Term Goals

Always have long-term goals. Every successful person has them – of course they have lists of short-term goals too – but it is the long-term goals that they are really interested in. Each day envision your main, long-term goal. This will in turn rewire the brain for more successful outcomes. So, start today!

Exercise

Exercise is a big motivator. It helps you to lose weight and get fitter; it helps to dispel depression; and it helps to drive you forward to do the things you want. We are designed to move, not sit in a chair all day, so go for walks; it's a great way to start getting fitter, and also to help you become more driven and motivated.

Diet

If you do not eat healthy foods then you may well feel tired and sluggish, and also have low energy levels and concentration problems. You should change your diet to include plenty of fruits and vegetables, as well as nuts (providing you do not have an allergy) and seeds, as well as good fats and plenty of plain water. Cut out bad fats and sugar. This will help you feel better and help to give you more energy to get out there and do more in your life.

Sleep

This is a big one to take care of if you are someone who does not sleep well! Lack of sleep has an impact on your energy levels and concentration. Without proper good quality sleep, you probably won't feel like completing your lists and reaching each goal. If you have tried everything and still cannot sleep – see your doctor – get this sorted out.

Mindset

Having the right mindset will make a huge difference to your progress. Doing some of the practices listed here or getting some help by using things like hypnotherapy, will help to change your mindset for the better. Some of the things I've listed here are well known for creating success and positivity in those who have seen a change, so do not hesitate to try them out and see for yourself how they may work for you. Getting in the right mindset is a must if you want the desired changes and help to reach your goals, so you should work hard at this every day. Successful people all have a great mindset, and this is one of the things that helps them to go on and achieve some amazing things. Some would say that having a positive mindset means that you're already halfway to achieving your goals.

In addition to the above, ask yourself these things:

Who am I, what is my passion, what is it I really need to do, and what is my higher calling?

Also, ask yourself – who will I become and what will that look like? The answers will come to you, and they will come to you a lot quicker if you have been doing some of the things suggested in this chapter. Whatever your dream is, be sure to enjoy the process of getting there, be determined, and be happy; don't stress out! Stressing yourself out about meeting targets and achieving certain goals within a fixed time scale will only make you anxious, angry, tired out, and even burnt out and will probably also make you a not very nice person to be around! This could happen if you're not prepared to be flexible with your goals and when things relating to your goals will be finished. Don't let that happen. Yes, you need a schedule and it's good to have a time scale in mind, but this also needs to be updated if needs be. Don't be too rigid in your thinking. There should be give and take, with a dash of patience added into the mix. Be happy that you are on your way to being a success. One step at a time.

- Get rid of any blocks or issues that you have, so that you are able to move forward.

- Don't be afraid to try therapy if you need the additional help.

- Learning new things rewires the brain – whole new

worlds, and new ways of thinking, will open up to you.

- Create a positive mindset.
- Read lots of books on self-development.
- If you need to work on yourself, and that's one of your goals, then make sure to do that before anything else. When you have done this, you will find yourself to be more effective when going forward to achieve your other goals.

So, it's safe to say that there are a few different methods you can try listed in this chapter, and the chances are that you will probably find one or two that will suit you.

"We must believe that we are gifted for something, and that this thing, at whatever cost, must be attained."
– Marie Curie

CHAPTER 7
Dream – Believe – Achieve

Fantastic – you have got a dream. If you can imagine, in detail, your dream goal and you have put together your lists – main list, steps list and micro-steps list – then you can start to do each of those steps to get to where you want to be. As you make progress with each of the steps, you will probably start to feel as if you are actually getting somewhere. That is because you ARE getting somewhere! It doesn't matter how small the steps are that you take, it is still a step forward. Keep that forward momentum going and over time you will be amazed at what you have achieved, and how far you have come. It is a really good feeling to be able to check off each of the things on your lists, and when you are feeling good about what it is you are doing, you then also start to believe that you can really do something awesome after all, in order to reach towards whatever your dream goal is, and you will enjoy the process as you complete each step. Always try to make it fun.

So, you have started to get things done and achieve some of the steps. Now would be a good time to make sure nothing is forgotten, and maybe put some post-it notes on your laptop, or your fridge, or wherever you think would be good, to serve as a constant reminder to do the next things on your lists. When you have finished a step or two, relax, unwind, and give yourself the credit you deserve, then continue with the next steps and continue on like this until you reach your goal.

Always have a goal, a dream, because sometimes people who stop dreaming or have no particular goals may find themselves leading empty lives. I say this because it is so important for people to always have goals and dreams; as humans we need this, so always have something to look forward to. It is exciting reaching goals, admittedly it is also sometimes challenging, but of course it is always worth it. Once you have reached your goal, don't allow yourself to fall back into boredom and those same old patterns again. Have new goals set for the future ahead of you. Create new habits in your life and you should find that changing a bad habit for a good and healthy habit brings you all sorts of benefits, including giving you more energy and confidence. And when you have more confidence you will find that you can usually achieve a lot more of the things that will make your life easier and more exciting! Believe in your dreams, believe you can achieve them, and take constant action towards that dream. If you really want to achieve your dream or goal you have to believe in it 110%. Imagining your dream in detail and believing that you can do it, whilst also having the self-belief that you can do these things, means that you are more likely to achieve them. The world is full of people who had dreams, but who also did not have the belief that they could do anything about it; so, they didn't do anything about it, and just dreamt about their goals instead of acting on them. Don't be one of those people. Sometimes making things happen in your world means taking a chance, taking some kind of risk, but that is necessary to get to where you want to be and to get to a place where you can reach that goal and say, "I did this, I made this happen". Also don't just hope for change or for your goals to just happen. Change your hoping to taking action. Only hoping is not something that will change everything by some miracle. You will need to create a new reality for yourself by changing "I hope" to "I believe it, so I can do it". If you are only passively hoping all the time, then that needs to change because it will lead you nowhere. If nothing has changed for you it's because you didn't believe it would, and you took no action. If you want to take a risk and do something outside of the normal box that you usually reside in, then the common reaction from other people might be "you can't do that, you'll lose out", or something similar. That's their fear talking. A lot of people have made important life decisions based on their fears. Think things through carefully and decide what it is that you are afraid of, then list those things. Now look at what you have written. How many things on your list make sense? How many could be changed over time and added to your goals list, and how many could you decide to change right now? Sometimes a fear is well founded, so you need to acknowledge that, but if it's a fear due to lacking in confidence for example, then it can be changed. You might have decided that you want to do something that exposes you to the world, and you fear the possible negative reactions to that and what other people might say. Then this is a fear your mind has conjured up to try and stop you from taking some kind of risk or doing something different. Anyway, if some people don't like what you are doing, that's ok because everyone is entitled to their opinion, and each person has their own likes and dislikes. That's fair enough. Should that stop you from achieving your goals though? Take me writing this book for instance, of course I wondered how it would be received out there in the big wide world but writing a book to help people is one of my main goals, so I overcame my fears and took massive action, and I wrote it anyway! I just went for it, and decided it was worth all of the work and risk. Of course, I hope that everyone will like it and find it useful, and I hope that people will get something great out of it. If it helps only a handful of people out there, then it will have been worth all of the work, and all the steps that I needed to complete in order to get this book published. There were a lot of steps! But I didn't give in because I believed in my goal of becoming an author and telling people all about this easy system that they can use to achieve their own goals.

- It's good to have dreams, but don't be a dreamer who never takes action.

- Believe in yourself and what you can do.

- Create new habits that will make it easier to progress with your lists.

- Progress with one step at a time, and you will see your goal begin to take shape right in front of you.

"Dream it – Believe it – Achieve it."
– Tony Robbins

CHAPTER 8
Affirmations for Success

A little more information on affirmations for you now. Speaking your chosen phrases helps you prepare yourself to take action and also helps to make the brain more resilient. You should repeat your chosen phrase for five minutes three times a day, on average, in order to attract the desired outcome and also help to rewire your brain so that it's able to drive you towards your dream goals and instil positivity. This process may take some time to be accepted in the subconscious mind. So, make sure to do this each day, and schedule to do so for a time when you know that you are going to be alone. I say this because it might be a bit embarrassing for some people to repeatedly say their affirmations out loud in front of partners, parents, children, co-workers etc, at different times every day. So, schedule saying your affirmations for when you are alone, or failing that, say them to yourself if there are a few people around. Although that's not ideal, because ideally you need to say them out loud. You could still repeat the affirmation to yourself a few times in between whatever tasks you are concentrating on. Do, however, avoid saying affirmations if you need to think about other things or are busy doing jobs that need your concentration. Do them in the quiet moments that you have to yourself. Even thinking the phrase will still help and have a rewiring effect on the brain after a certain amount of time and under certain circumstances. Remember, we are what we think, so always think positively. What you are doing by thinking or saying your affirmations (preferably saying them out loud) repeatedly is reconditioning yourself; reconditioning yourself to have the confidence that you will need to take a certain desired step. When we have learnt that we can do something new after all, then this will also have a rewiring effect on us and help to make us more able to move on to the next steps on our lists and achieve them too. A new you will begin to emerge with a 'yes, I can do this' attitude.

Also, don't think things like 'I wish I was more successful', because wishing is not doing. Instead think 'I will become more successful and complete my lists.' The emphasis should be on taking action.

Here are some more examples:

'I will eat healthily; I will lose weight.'

'I will pass my driving test; I have got this.'

'I will attract love and respect into my life.'

'My goals are becoming a reality; I achieve them easily.'

'Today I am confident and will ask my boss for a raise, I deserve this.'

'I am a successful person.'

'I no longer smoke horrid cigarettes. I don't need them.'

'I will get my dream job; I've got this.'

'I will do my exercise today, as planned. It feels great.'

'I am a great, unique and marvellous person.'

'I will take steps towards my goal – I will (add the name of the goal and which steps you are taking to achieve it).'

'I am calm, I am strong, I can do this.'

'I am happy, and I feel so confident.'

'I attract wealth into my life.'

'I am super confident.'

'I will accomplish anything that I set my mind to.'

Start writing out some of your own affirmations, then begin to say them to yourself every day. Saying them out loud is best and is thought to have a better outcome. This in turn will begin to make a real difference, and help you get into the right mindset to go and take action, and when you take action, guess what, good things start to happen in your world. There is a lot of research regarding saying affirmations and it's something that will help you to accomplish more. This technique is especially effective when teamed with other goal setting techniques, such as visualisation. So, you could choose to say your desired phrase out loud and at the same time imagine that it is happening in detail. The harder you visualise, and the more details that you put into it, the better it will be. This image and command should eventually be accepted by the subconscious mind, and after about 25-30 days the brain will have rewired in order to accept and focus on the desired goal. Whatever the subconscious mind accepts has to be acted on. HOWEVER, and this is important, if the deeper mind believes a long-held, deeply rooted negative belief, then affirmations may not work, because affirmations target the conscious mind first, and not the subconscious initially, so if what you are saying to yourself is in conflict with a deeply held negative belief then it may result in an inner struggle. In this case it's necessary to remove those negative subconscious learnings first, with therapies such as hypnosis. If you are saying things like 'I am super confident' and experience has taught you that you are not actually confident, then you won't believe what you are saying! So, you must be sure to believe in the thing that you're asking for and believe that it's possible. If you have low self-esteem or depression, you must sort this out and overcome these things first.

Affirmations can give you more confidence and help to rewire the brain over a long period of time, and will also help you make a start towards something, but they also take time to sink in. At some stage you will have to take actions yourself to bring about the changes that you want. Thinking and saying what it is you want from life is all well and good, but without taking real actions, you won't get far. So, yes, say affirmations to help PREPARE you for your goals, and really believe in what you tell yourself, then go out there and make sure that you actually do it.

So, to recap:

- Affirmations may take 25-30 days to be accepted by the subconscious mind – providing there is not a deeply held, contradictory, negative belief.

- Do them for five minutes, three times a day.

- Repeat them often and believe in what you are telling yourself.

- They might not work for everyone, especially if you are someone who has low self-esteem, or you are depressed. Work on sorting out these issues first; make overcoming these issues your main goal.

- Affirmations challenge self-sabotaging and negative thoughts.

- Affirmations need practice in order to make long lasting changes.

- Get a notebook especially for all of your affirmations. Keep this for your eyes only.

- All statements you say to yourself should be positive.

- Use affirmations alongside other techniques, like visualisation, for better results.

- If accepted by the subconscious mind, the positive statements you tell yourself can be acted upon a lot more easily.

It might take a bit of time to make a difference in your life, but aren't you worth it? Yes, of course you are. This is another technique that you now have in your toolkit to help with self-motivation and being successful in trying out the steps required to reach your goals.

"In order to carry a positive action we must
develop here a positive vision."
– Dalai Lama

CHAPTER 9
Future Pacing

I thought that it would also be helpful to include a little bit of information about something called future pacing, and also explain a bit more about visualisation. Future pacing is a technique that is used by most hypnotherapists and NLP's (neuro-linguistic practitioners) and is something that should be included in most sessions. To explain it simply, you would mentally rehearse a future situation, or a result that you're wanting to achieve, so that the desired outcome automatically happens. Therapists will use this technique to test if the client feels okay with the changes that would be put in place. Through the use of this technique, a therapist and their client will then be able to achieve a much better result. The client will be able to visualise their future in a positive way and will be more likely to reach their goal, or their desired way of being, or even be more able to deal with certain situations.

Future pacing gives the brain positive images, sounds and feelings that will help to make success much more likely. Each time the client mentally rehearses a situation, or future paces it, the situation then becomes easier for them and the client also gains confidence.

Remember to always picture the future in a positive way. Whether or not you are having hypnosis or future pacing, you should still try some of the points listed below within your daily life to help you in bringing about the changes you want.

- Visualise what your future will look like.

- Connect with professionals who can help you to see what

a great future would be like.

- See a hypnotherapist or NLP practitioner and try future pacing to get you past any negative blocks or negative ways of thinking about your future, or even to help you see yourself as you will be after giving up bad habits etc.

- Never have negative thoughts about the future. If you are having these kinds of thoughts, then you should examine why and take action to stop them.

- Try keeping a gratitude journal, and only allow good, positive comments. What are you grateful for today?

- Know your weaknesses and work on them so that they do not affect you in the future; imagine yourself without these issues.

- Visualise yourself in a year's time, or whenever it is, having completed your goal or goals. How do you feel, how do you look, what will you have achieved? Imagine this and do so often.

Seeing your future in a positive way and working hard towards your goals, making your lists and persisting with each step on the way up the ladder, should work towards giving you a much better chance of getting more of what you want in life. Visualising is a good daily practice. Imagine what you want and make sure that you do so in detail, that is an important point here, you have to see every detail in order for this to be effective. There are a lot of professionals who practice these techniques, and it has helped them in all sorts of ways so that they are able to reach their goals. The more they imagined something, the more it started to happen for them, almost like magic! I have tried this myself, and I can tell you that it does work. Slowly but surely things start to shift, and then what you are imagining does start to happen! If you are visualising great, positive outcomes then that's what you should end up with in all likelihood, however, the opposite is true as well; if you are thinking about a lot of negative things, then guess what, that's what you will end up having in your life!

Only a tiny percentage of people practice visualisation regularly, but most of those who do find that it really works for them, when it is done in the right way and is done consistently. In order to make the positive change that you are building up in your mind's eye, you will need to practice visualisation every day. Start with something small that is familiar to you and begin to change the details of that image into what you want it to be. It's a bit like decorating a house and seeing how a room will look after you have finished painting and wallpapering, the new rugs, the furniture etc. There are, however, some people who find it hard to visualise images, unfortunately if that is the case this technique won't work for you, so instead you could try putting together a vision board to see if that will help. You can look at it every day to remind yourself of what it is that you want to achieve. I have a friend who can't imagine her life any other way than how it has always been, her life is a bit chaotic to say the least, and guess what her life stayed the same – she couldn't imagine it any other way, so it didn't change. So, begin to use visualisation and in turn help yourself to get a better balance in your life and help with whatever it is you are striving for. Try this out for yourself; it is just one more simple step to help you push towards your future goals. Keep going, step by step.

"It is not the mountain we conquer, but ourselves."
– Sir Edmund Hillary

CHAPTER 10
Bigger Steps

When you have completed the micro-steps and the main steps, you will then find yourself within reach of one of your main goals. Perhaps you have already achieved it? Well done, give yourself a pat on the back. The bigger the steps that you complete and the more ambitions that you achieve, the more satisfying it is and the more motivated you feel. When you have made a start and you have begun taking those micro-steps, and then the bigger steps that are needed, you will then find that there is a huge psychological benefit and you have taken action and can see the future taking shape – a future that you have imagined for so long. As you work on each micro-step, and get ever closer to the bigger steps, and you take those bigger steps, and you then complete your goal, you will then see that it is a 'wow' moment. It's fantastic. It's such a great feeling, to be achieving more and more and this in turn also leads to an increase in your confidence and self-worth.

Breaking down each of your main goals into much smaller steps is very important. Many people think that they will never be able to reach their goals; it just seems too daunting, it's too much work. It can be difficult to know where to start, so most people just do not follow their dreams and ambitions, instead they just give up. But now that you know how it can be possible to help yourself towards achieving your goal, through this book for instance and all the suggestions I am giving you, you are now on your way – hopefully – to reaching all of your dreams. Never think that you cannot do this. This really is a simple way of helping you get to where you need to be in life. People who write their task lists down get things done. Fact! There has been research into list makers, and how successful they are compared to non-list makers. The list makers and goal setters were miles ahead of those who didn't write these lists, and they had also often achieved a lot more in their lives compared to the non-list makers who had achieved very little in comparison. Unfortunately, many people don't bother to try this. It sometimes doesn't even occur to them.

Taking bigger steps may be scary, but unless you do it and put yourself out there, nothing will ever change. Yes, you may be afraid to make a start towards that dream goal of yours, but when you think about it you have already started by deciding to buy this book, and by following this method and the helpful guidelines that it contains. So, your first step is already done. It's also amazing how much information there is on the internet, you can research anything. You could read books and look at tutorials on YouTube for instance. There really is so much that you can do to find out more about your interests and find the information you will need to reach you chosen goal. However, it is a sad fact that a lot of people will not use these resources to better themselves, or to help them find out how to do something they have always wanted to do. So, learning new things and doing your research is vital, and usually it is also necessary in order to take bigger steps towards your new future. In the beginning you will probably have to spend a fair amount of time researching, but it's so worth it, so never skip this part of the work that you need to do to complete a step. Of course, there are other things that you will need to know as well – there will be more on this later on in the book. When taking bigger steps to a goal, however, it is important to bear in mind the following things:

- Do not let negative conditioning hold you back from your dreams. This can also include things we have grown up with, such as being taught: "know your place", and "children should be seen and not heard", and "respect your elders", or other negative beliefs such as: "you aren't good enough".

- Be kind to yourself – you are putting yourself out there and taking some risks, which may feel a bit scary to you at first. So, congratulate yourself for taking action and for getting out of your box!

- Have a voice, be heard, be brave and know that taking steps will lead you to that place you want to be.

- Have confidence in your abilities.

- Place post-it notes or make cards to put around your house, as a way of reminding you what your current step is.

- Put a big sign/card next to your bed stating what your goal is. It should be the first thing you see in the morning.

- Be prepared to make mistakes; learn from them. We all make mistakes, especially when we are doing something new that we have never attempted before. It's a learning process. Those mistakes are still valuable and can teach you a lot about what didn't work and why.

- When you've achieved a big step, treat yourself in some way – you did it. Way to go!

- Be authentic.

- Don't be afraid of what people will say/think of you. Doing so will only hold you back. Seriously, this is a big drawback. If you want to get on in your life, then you must get over this and push yourself to take action, and yes stick your head up out of your box and be prepared to take some negativity from folks. This hopefully won't happen to you, but if it does, be prepared with a response of some kind – keep that response positive.

- Keep smiling.

- Keep on keeping on.

- Enjoy the feeling of each accomplishment – you deserve it. Well done!

- Never throw away the information that you have on any of your lists, even if it's something that didn't work. Keep all of your lists safe.

- Make one of your steps/goals to be something that revolves around helping others. Doing this makes you happy, as well as the other person. Helping other people in some way or another gives you a warm inner glow – it feels so good! It makes a difference to that person's life and it might even mean that they start achieving their goals because of something you've helped them with. Good vibes! Good karma!

- Build up your self-esteem without needing the approval of others. If you need to work on this then it will take time, but it will also get easier as you progress. Stick with it.

- Each big step is another building block in your master plan.

Remember that all of your hard work, no matter how long it takes, still has the payoff waiting at the end of it all for you. Some people may think that achieving goals this way is boring, and they cannot see how it will work for them. Yes, it does require some work especially in the beginning, with the list making and the research, but once that is all in place, it becomes easier and should be pretty straightforward for you to do. Using this method to reach your goals isn't complicated. Ask yourself, what is it that could possibly be boring about reaching your goal? What has worked for you so far? I am assuming that not a lot has, otherwise you wouldn't be reading this book. There are a wide range of methods and programmes out there, admittedly, but ask yourself how many of those have this level of research behind them, and how many have a good track record of successful outcomes at the end of it. Some might do, and some might not. I often wonder why it is that more people don't follow this way of achieving a task and reaching a goal or dream, I can't answer that unfortunately because I have no idea! Perhaps they don't know about it, or perhaps it's because it's such a simple thing to do, that they don't believe it would work. If so, then it's a shame that they don't know about it or are not trying it for whatever reason. But you know about it don't you, and that puts you ahead of the crowd. After all, you have nothing to lose by trying this method, and everything to gain.

"A goal without a plan is just a wish."
– Antoine de Saint-Exupéry

CHAPTER 11
Mistakes – Move Past Them

Sometimes you will likely make mistakes when you are trying to complete a goal in your life. Mistakes happen, it is part of the learning process and it is important that you do not let them interrupt your journey, by giving up or being put off from doing something because you failed this time. Perhaps it has made you feel a bit down and has affected your confidence. Sometimes the mistake is not your fault; maybe you have put your trust in someone and they have let you down or given you the wrong information. This goes back to checking people out and doing your research on anything you have been advised to do, to see if it is indeed the correct information. Always double check all of the information anyway to ensure that it is okay to proceed with, then add this information to your lists, once you know that it all checks out.

I know it is not always easy to overcome mistakes, as you have invested your time and resources into something that did not work out or was not right in some way. This can be annoying and even soul-destroying. Treat it as a lesson learnt and find out what should have been done and how is best to get back on track again. If you do not get back on track, then you will be stuck where you are, and your progress will stop. Try to learn from any mistakes, you are human, you are fallible, it happens. We all make mistakes; this is part of life. It is important, however, that you forgive yourself and move forward. Try not to dwell on what has happened. Turn your mistakes into a positive thing, because they have shown you what doesn't work, and you can learn what to avoid the next time around.

When you make a mistake or fail at something, do not think:

'Oh, I've tried, I'll have to give up now', instead think to yourself: 'Okay, this time I'll ask the right people, do more research and try a different approach or tactic.' A mistake is part of your past experiences, forgive yourself and accept that you cannot change it. Use the life lessons you have learnt, file them, forget them, and move forward with your plans to succeed. Many of the top professionals fail time and time again, they all make mistakes of some kind, but they do not let these mistakes hold them back from moving forward with their plans. They never give up – never. Their level of self-confidence and their determination is just plain awesome! This is one of the main reasons why the people who are top of their field of expertise are the ones who succeed in life. They never give up; they are constantly doing things that further their plans to succeed and reach their goals. Of course, they also recognise when something is not working and adjust their approach accordingly, or they may even start all over again, or switch to another goal entirely.

In the end, some goals are just not possible, no matter how hard you try or what resources you throw at it. So, always be honest when writing your lists as to what may be achievable and what is not, based on your own circumstances. For example, there is no way I am going to run a marathon, I am not fit enough, and I also have asthma; it is out of the question for me to do this, no matter how much I might want to, or dream about how great it would be. Of course, that does not mean that I cannot get fitter, but it would have to be done slowly and I would have to know the limits in relation to my case and stick to walking! You must accept your strengths and weaknesses and work with them. Try to improve on your weaknesses if you can, but always with your own limits and safety in mind. Some people will disagree with this and will say that you need to break your limits, but these people may also be very fit people already.

Your dream goal might not be something that is a physical activity, such as running. Perhaps you want to give up smoking and eating bad foods. These sorts of goals are achievable, but there are others that just won't be. We all need to recognise that this is sometimes the case and then base our goals on our own personal circumstances. Circumstances can be changed of course, over time, but some cannot be changed, and you will simply have to work with them.

A fantasy is just that – a fantasy. All professionals recognise that and do not waste any time on goals that are simply unattainable. Perhaps it could also be the case that a major mistake in your past is holding you back and maybe it has affected your confidence, either through a fault of your own, or someone else's. Do not let these major life downers throw a spanner into the workings of your life. Forgive yourself. Apologise if you need to. Come to terms with it. Get some help if you need to, and never be ashamed to ask for help either, that is just silly and will leave you stuck in a cycle of misery. No-one wants that. Take action to sort out any past mistakes that are holding you back – own them. Then move towards your brighter future. If another person's actions have left you feeling ashamed or depressed, or feeling like you are not capable of reaching and achieving any goals, then that is not your fault, nor is it your responsibility and that is something that the other person needs to own. Do not allow the negativity of the past to drag you down in your life and result in self-pity, blame, guilt and even anger. These emotions will hold you back big time. To allow yourself to be held back by the past is a mistake in itself. Whatever happened acknowledge it and move on. Use any kind of mistake or negative event as a driver to push you on towards achieving your goals and completing all of your lists. Forge your foundation into something that is very strong; something that can be used to propel you towards success and progress on to reach your goals. Realise that everyone makes mistakes and all you need to do is draw a line under them and learn from them. Look at it like: 'Okay, that did not work, what is next?' You need to have self-belief, so that if you do make a mistake of some kind, you don't just give up, and you instead become the kind of person who will quickly get over a mistake and not let it stop you from moving forward. The most successful leaders in the world are the ones who are able to brush off any mistakes or interruptions that cross their path on their way to achieving a goal or task, it's how they think. Their brains are just wired this way, so it's easier for them to carry on with something, and not allow any negativity to creep in and halt their plans. Sure, they can get annoyed or upset about any mistakes or hold ups they encounter, but they also get on with finding a solution as soon as possible. The road ahead may have many obstacles for you to overcome, but most people will have to face this when they are trying to get to a better place. You are a goal setter. An achiever, a winner. That's what you are! Winners don't give up, they have a certain determination; a fire that's lit from within, and many things may have stoked this inner fire. Many successful people had childhoods that were not ideal and perhaps were told they would never amount to anything. This then in turn made them want to show everyone that they were wrong about them, and that they can in fact turn their hand to many things and be a success. Whatever has happened to hold you back – a delay, an error, a past event, or anything else that it may be – you need to get yourself to the same level of determination as these driven professionals, and light your inner fire as well, and then you can continue onwards with your goals. The past is the past, and you should not let it dictate your future. I have personally known quite a few people who could not get past mistakes of some kind, and they let it ruin a large part of their lives, they had years and years of self-inflicted pain and self-doubt that they needlessly endured. They were so miserable – what a waste, their lives could have been so much happier, all they needed to do was move on from those past mistakes. So, it's necessary to come to terms with your mistakes and move past them, whatever kind they were or are - big ones or little tiny ones. The future is yet to be determined by you and you alone must travel that road.

"Tomorrow is another day."
– Scarlett O'Hara, Gone with the Wind

CHAPTER 12
Motivation

There may be days when you feel absolutely fine and you have plenty of time to complete some of the steps that are on your lists, you even have everything set up and ready to go ahead and then for some reason you feel as though you just can't be bothered.

Okay, so this is pretty normal, we all have days where we feel like this, I know that I certainly do. If this happens it is normally a case of getting back that self-motivation because for whatever reason, on days like this we don't have any motivation and we can't be bothered to get on with what we need to do; we just want to do nothing. So, what you need to do is find that self-motivation again, but how do we do this? Here are some ideas:

- Remind yourself why you're doing a task, visualise the goal in your mind and see it and see yourself achieving it.

- Make a start on your steps and after a few minutes you should find that it gets easier.

- Go for a short walk to 'wake up' a bit; sometimes fresh air and exercise are all that you need.

- Is your step too big right now? Cut it down into smaller pieces to make it less daunting.

- If you are distracted or busy with other things, delegate some of your tasks.

- Fear of completing a step can stop you from getting on

with it. What is it you fear? Get help – hypnosis maybe – so you can move past this block or you could try a different therapy or technique like the ones I have already mentioned in this book.

- Talk to someone who motivates you, ask them about getting going again. Could your friends or family help you out?

- Have a routine each day and schedule in your task time, so you always know what is when.

- Read about the things you want to do; listen to podcasts etc, to help motivate you.

- Make sure nothing slows down your progress. What are the things that do slow you down? Fix them.

- Try not to get frustrated if a step goes wrong, or will not work, or nothing happens, or if something takes ages to happen and sort out. It happens, recognise that, it is part of the journey. Don't give up, just be patient. Adjust your approach.

- Remember your affirmations. These will remind you to carry on and persist with your goals.

- Once you have started a task, the finish is then that much closer. When you have successfully completed a task, you will find that you feel more motivated to continue. Doing things that you enjoy or doing things that you are passionate about is motivating in itself. If your day is filled with boring stuff to get through – 'Oh no, is my ironing pile that big?' – then delegate or find a way to do these things in a manner that won't drag you down and de-motivate you. Listening to music whilst doing boring tasks can help, also creating a schedule for certain boring tasks is also a good idea. Remember your goals are not going anywhere, they will still be with you no matter what distractions you have, or what days off you have. You just have to realise that sometimes you will need to motivate yourself to get going again. Be truthful with yourself, what was it that started the idea that became your goal? What led up to the idea? Are you doing it for yourself or someone else?

- What inspires you the most? Are you looking to improve your life so that you can earn more and give more to your family in terms of time and possessions? Is it a famous person who inspired you to begin your journey? What was it about them that first caught your eye, or your imagination? Always have a role model to look up to as your inspiration.

- Find your sense of purpose and remind yourself of what it is when you are lacking motivation.

Having a sense of purpose in life can be the motivating factor for some people if they don't already have one. This is very important. Knowing that you have a reason to get up in the morning and that you have something to strive for is a vital part of life. If you feel like you do not have a sense of purpose, then don't worry that is something you can change. Find a purpose, find a hobby, find an idea, and plan a goal. Everyone should have a purpose, something you really want to be doing to deliver an outcome that benefits you and your family in the best possible ways. The most successful people on the planet will also have days where they cannot motivate themselves enough to achieve their goals, but they know of different ways to pick themselves up again and begin the task in hand. Sometimes that can be hard to do, but they do not give up.

Motivation may mean different things to different people, for instance some people may find that they use failure as a way to drive them on. Each failure is seen as another reason as to why they have to carry on and prove to themselves that it can be done, and they don't like to admit defeat. They feel like they have to win. Another motivator is taking responsibility for your life. This is important as you should be able to design your life as you see fit; you are in charge of it and you need to become the leader, not the one who is led. Then there is another one that needs to be addressed – mortality. What would you want to achieve if these were your last days on earth? What kind of things would you wish you had done? We all have a short time on this earth, and we need to remember this and achieve our goals whilst we can. Then there is, of course, another kind of motivation that a lot of successful people have – hunger. Sometimes people want to reach a goal in their lives so much that they can almost taste it! They really want it, and it takes up so much of their time thinking about it, talking about it, and dreaming about it as well. Basically, it's a very strong desire that can lead to eventual success, as these hungry people usually don't give up easily. Actually, if you combined all of these types of motivation you would be on to a winner. Be hungry for your dream, use any failures to drive you on, be aware of your time on this planet, and take responsibility for your dream – be the captain of your own destiny. This sounds like a recipe for success to me. You need to acquire the right mindset to be able to do the same as the successful person does. Do you want to continue in the same old way as always or do you want to get out there and achieve things that will lead to improving your lot in life? Only you can answer this.

I have known of a few people who could not motivate themselves, and of course that meant that nothing ever changed for them. Everything stayed the same and any goals that they may have had were not reached, because they thought it was too hard to start taking action and instead, they basically gave up before they had ever begun. Never underestimate the power and importance of self-motivation, you are going to need a lot of it to make the thing you want to achieve happen; things like creating your lists, and taking those steps one at a time, they are things that require self-motivation. No one else can do it for you, you must believe that you can do what you set your mind to and be excited about what you are aiming for, and when you are excited about a project you become the motivated person that you need to be; you take ACTION, and then what happens is the things in your life start to evolve and change, and that's really exciting.

"The path to success is to take massive determined action."
– Tony Robbins

CHAPTER 13
Your Schedule

Being the best at something and reaching these exciting goals, of course, means giving it 100% and you will obviously need to be dedicated and single-minded in your approach to each goal and you must also have a certain 'can do' mindset in order to maintain your progress towards each goal step by step. You will also need something else – a schedule.

Reaching goals will of course require you to set aside a certain amount of time each day, so that you are able to do what is needed. It could be that you just need 20 minutes a day, or maybe you will need a couple of hours a day, to work on your step or steps. Whatever is needed you are going to need to schedule in time just for you. There could be interruptions or other things that come up that will mean you cannot do more that day; it happens, that's life! You can just pick up where you left off, whenever you are able to get back to your work; by work I mean your work on your lists and steps towards your goals and ambitions. So many people who are trying to achieve their goals have not put a schedule together for themselves and instead try to get things done in a haphazard way, then when very little, if anything, happens they then begin to wonder why! Add putting a schedule together for yourself to the top of your lists as one of the steps that's needed.

By scheduling in time for your work, you are much more likely to get it done and dusted and progress onto the next thing needed on the ladder to a successful outcome. If you live with a partner or have children, maybe they could help you by doing some of the chores you would normally do, thus creating a bit more free time each day. If that is not possible, then look at your day as a whole and decide what needs to go, or can go, from your current schedule each day. Perhaps you could do simple things like getting up half an hour earlier and going to bed an hour later, or maybe one less evening out and instead spending it training or doing something towards whatever it is you are aiming for. You could also look at how to cut back on things like surfing the internet, other than for research purposes, obviously don't cut back on your researching, which will probably be done in large part on the internet. Answer a smaller number of emails, have your shopping delivered instead of spending two hours in a supermarket doing it yourself. Could someone else mow the lawn for you? It could be anything where you might save yourself some time. There will be loads of small things that can add up to give you a lot more time to yourself. Look at all the ways you can make time each day, or each week, and you will find that they will soon all add up. Then you can schedule in the time that you have saved as time that you can spend doing your steps or work.

It is straightforward really; it's definitely not rocket science. When you have written down your goals and scheduled in your work time, then things will begin to change, and things get done. If you do not schedule in your work time, then you will find steps are not being done and are perhaps also discarded or are not looked into, because you do not have the time, you do not know when you will have the time and then it will mean progress is slow or at a standstill. When that happens, you may decide to give up entirely. DO NOT let that happen – always have a schedule! Making time and sticking to schedules means you will need to have a certain amount of discipline, but oh boy, when you reach those goals it is totally worth it. Then you will see that all the work you have done has brought you the success that you deserve. It clicks – it is a lightbulb moment – the formula you followed worked. Hey, how about that! Having a routine lowers stress levels as well, as you know when you will have the time to do your steps and you will also know when you can relax and take it easy. You can try starting a 30-day schedule challenge, where you change around your normal routine to suit you better and allow more time for the other things you want to do, give it those 30 days to see how it works out for you. Also bear in mind that not all routines are created equally, look closely at what needs to go, and what things are dragging you down in some way. If you've had the same routine for years, then it's more than likely time to switch things up. A rearrangement of your normal routine may well be a good thing, ask yourself what is it that you currently dislike the most, and stop doing that or delegate it to someone else. If that's not possible, then maybe you could consider outsourcing that particular thing. Of course, you will always have to prioritise the most important tasks as the ones that you do first, there's no getting around this! Setting a time of the day or evening when you know you are able to get things done for yourself is essential. Make it fun, write out your new schedule on coloured card and pin it up somewhere, and buy some pretty notebooks for your research. How does your home office area look? Maybe you don't have one. Find a corner of your home to set up a small desk for your laptop and notebooks, and anything else you will need to have close by. If you have a home office already, how organised is it? A tidy well organised office area makes your work easier to do – a tidy organised office means a tidy organised mind!

You could also put together a vision board, many people find this helps them to focus on a future goal. A vision board will start to make things you've been dreaming about seem more real, because it's right there in front of you every day, for you to look at and remind yourself why you are doing things and how you will be, or what you will have done when you reach your goals and ambitions. You could choose to include photos of whatever it is you're aiming to do, or magazine cuttings, or maybe even newspaper articles and inspirational quotes – it could also be useful to include a timeline. You could pin up a small card with, complete my goal – add in what goal the goal is – in 6 months, or whatever timescale it is that you are using. There doesn't need to be anything plain or boring about your lists either, they can look exciting: buy colourful A4 notebooks, use stickers or write in various colours of pens and pencils. If you're good at drawing, make meaningful drawn images of your goals, and tasks if you like; for instance, you may be overweight, and have drawn a picture of yourself as a thin person! Or drawn a picture of a place you want to visit. Whatever it is you want, there are so many different mediums that you could use to make a great vision board. When you have done all this, it will look so much more interesting and it will come alive! You will see things are starting to come together and things will begin to progress further for you. Sorting out your schedule should be easy when it is organised in the right way, and this is definitely a necessary step in the journey to succeeding. Don't underestimate the necessity for personal time to yourself to get your work started and continued until you have taken all the steps that you need to. If you lead a very busy life, with lots going on, then you will have to accept that some things will need to go, or that they will need to be re-arranged, or as I've said previously, they can be outsourced; perhaps you have small children and you are very busy? Then think about getting family to help out or getting a babysitter? Lots of people use outsourcing to free up some of their time. This could especially apply to you if you have a busy schedule, but there are lots of companies that will take over some of the work for you. Of course, this will cost money. If money is an issue, then you will need to look closely at what you can do to have a schedule that will fit in with your current lifestyle. When you have found the extra time, you can then get on with all of those wonderful steps. Your time is precious, so use it wisely.

"Either I will find a way, or I will make one."
– Sir Philip Sidney

CHAPTER 14
Social Media

Most people have joined one or more social media platforms. If you already have an online presence it will be easier to find goal related information through your friends and followers, or by reading other people's pages and posts. These sites can be a goldmine of information. There are also various groups you can join too. If you are on Facebook, then join as many groups that are relating to your area of interest as you can. It will then be easy for you to ask questions and join in on conversations in these groups which should lead to all sorts of helpful information and in turn will make your steps easier, this will then take you closer to completing the current steps you are working on.

A word of advice here; often if you ask a question you will get several answers all of which will be giving different advice, or maybe there will only be two or three answers saying the same thing. Always take advice from the experts who have been there and have already done it, not so much from the newbies. Check out people's profiles and pages to see what kind of thing they are doing, how well they seem to be doing, and how long they have been doing it for. At the end of the day though, it is up to you – when taking advice – to choose what you feel will be the right approach for your particular circumstances and your current level of expertise, and whose advice you would like to follow. Whose advice is it that makes the most sense to you? Not everyone wants to be on a social media platform, I know that some people, especially older people, do not particularly want to join social media platforms. But I would urge you to try it out if you're not already on one, because it will make a difference to you and allow you to make all sorts of contacts. It's a good thing to speak to people outside of your usual circle, as they can give you all kinds of useful feedback, advice, and support. Yes, there can also be negative experiences on these platforms, as not everyone on there is who they seem to be. But if you ever have any problems, then it's easy to block them from your account so that they cannot contact you again. I have had one or two people who have been a problem, and in the end, I just blocked them. I know these kinds of experiences have driven some women away and they have chosen to leave the sites altogether. This is a pity, as there is so much to learn and enjoy on these sites. So, don't let any negatives put you off if you ever do have this kind of thing happen to you, that would mean that they have won and that's what they want. There are far too many things that can benefit you on social media to ever be put off. Your goals that you are working on, or perhaps promoting something, or keeping in touch with family and friends, all of this makes it worth staying on these sites.

Do not rush, always be sure to do your research on any experts to see if they are actually someone who checks out in every way, and also someone who you could take advice from, as sometimes experts are not all that they seem. Beware of advertised 'freebies'; they often lead to a course of some sort which you will undoubtedly have to pay for. Similarly, be aware of free downloads that ask for your email, a name, or an address. They are not all scammers, of course, but be wary of giving out too much personal information about yourself.

Networking on social media sites is one of the main ways to build contacts and even partnerships in this current digital age.

It is usually good if used in the right ways, to build your business brand and drive clients to your website, for example. You could also develop a friendship with someone else on a social media site, someone with similar goals, and you could support each other in your new ventures and regularly report to one another about how you are getting on with those goals; this drives you to meet more targets and keep on track, as you will be motivating each other. It is also good to have someone else to talk to about the things that interest you, which perhaps your family or friends don't particularly know about or have an interest in. Social media is a great way to find lots of likeminded people who will understand where you are coming from and will share similar ambitions. When you have these wonderful business/interest's buddies, it really does make things seem that little bit easier, as you then have someone to share all the ups and downs of your similar goals with. Someone to empathise with, to laugh with, to solve problems with, and someone to celebrate with, and of course someone who you can learn from.

Here are some of the main reasons to be on social media sites:

- Find a mentor to help guide you.

- Engage with any customers, provide support and tell them about your services.

- Promote yourself, your ideas, and your goals.

- Make lifelong friends.

- Be able to be more creative.
- Shy people can express ideas more easily.
- Showcase your expertise via images, posts, and also videos.
- Use social media for a marketing campaign or to raise awareness around your ideas or products. A lot of marketing, if done in the right way, on social media can be very effective.
- You can get useful feedback from people about your ideas.

Being on various platforms can be an enormous help to you but do also remember that it will take time to build up a presence and find the right people.

"You cannot swim for new horizons until you
have courage to lose sight of the shore."
– William Faulkner

CHAPTER 15
Make Your World Bigger

If you want to reach any goal then you will have to make your world bigger, whether that is just a little bit bigger or a lot bigger will of course depend on the goal you are aiming for. How exactly do you make your world bigger then?

Just by doing your lists, you will probably find that you are already doing things you would not normally do. For example, you may be reading more than usual, taking courses, doing research, joining clubs and organisations, contacting more people – some of whom may be top professionals – maybe you're even meeting them either in person or via web conferencing; just generally thinking outside of the box and learning new things means that you are probably doing things that you wouldn't normally do.

When you do these kinds of things and plan for a better future, you are starting to expand your world by adding in different experiences to those that you are used to. If you are thinking of your life, and your current situation, and what you want in your world then you now know that by adding in these new experiences you are basically putting more air in your bubble. The air in your bubble is the new experiences, and the more experiences you have and the more tasks you have completed on your lists, then the more air that will be pushed into your bubble and the bigger your world gets. So, adding things to your life; lists, tasks, experiences etc, means you will be less afraid to take some (safe) risks, or step outside of your usual box. Successful goal setters have very big bubbles. Their bubbles are growing every day, and with every new experience they have.

Remember, start small and build up gradually.

Lots of people have started with small steps and gradually they have forged a path to their goal, bit by bit, step by step. It is important not to do the bigger steps when starting out. Do not go at it full throttle, hell for leather, steaming ahead at full speed, because you will miss something out or make mistakes of some kind. Of course, there are people out there who have done it all fast and they have got lucky, but I think they are in the minority. Don't trust to luck: 'Oh, I'll wait for it to happen...' instead put in the work and take it slow as you move forward at a steady pace, learning everything you need to know along the way, learning properly from the right sources. These sources being the experts, or people you know who have already reached the goal that you want to reach as well.

Try making your own luck by doing a proper job on things like research, and you should find that things will then progress as they should. Perhaps you might have to wait longer to reach a goal, because anything worthwhile usually takes longer to do, but keep on keeping on and you will get there.

So, what should we be aiming for?

- New experiences to help make your world bigger. Try out new things that you have wanted to do for ages and start with the small things first.

- The more 'air' in your bubble, the more your world is growing.

- Adding to your bubble makes you less afraid to take (safe) risks.

- Do different things, have different experiences, learn new things, add to your bubble.

- Do not rush your lists, you might miss something important, take it steady and check everything through properly: research and research again.

- Don't rely on being lucky and it just happening for you, make your own luck by working for it step by step. Luck is being in the right place at the right time, and so few of us are, so make things happen yourself, this will help you grow in confidence.

- Don't be afraid to leave your box – you can do it! If you are afraid, it will mean you cannot reach any goals. Think about the last time you did something a bit brave to achieve something you wanted to do, and it meant that you had to leave your comfort zone. I bet that when you had done it, even if you felt a bit uncomfortable whilst you were doing it, I am sure when you had completed whatever it was, that you were so happy you had taken that step and gone through with it. Remember how that felt. Learn that you are capable of doing things that take you outside of your usual realm of experience.

- Enjoy new experiences and be brave. This adds to your world and expands it.

- List makers enjoy more success – by far. This is a fact. Write out your lists in as much detail as you can, do not miss out even the smallest step.

- Knowledge is power. Nothing could be truer. The more knowledge you have under your belt the better, become an expert at whatever you are trying to achieve. So much so that you could eventually pass on your expertise to others and help them out, this will also increase your bubble and make you feel good.

You should be aiming to have a shake-up of your routines, if you have had the same one for as long as you can remember; the same thing over and over again is boring and the monotony is soul destroying as well, for anyone who is constantly allowing this to be a normal part of their lives and putting up with the same old thing all of the time. If this is you, then you are not adding air to your bubble. By staying in the same routine, you are effectively keeping your world smaller than it should be. Examine what you do every day, ask yourself why it is staying the same, how can you begin to change it? Try doing something different or doing something you already do differently. A shake-up will activate your brain and re-engage you with life. You don't want to burn out from the boredom! That would be awful and so unnecessary, so find ways to experience new things, as adding in these new experiences allows you to become fully engaged, and also energised, and then guess what? You become more enthusiastic. Life then becomes more meaningful, and so when that happens you want to get out there and get stuff done, which in turn puts even more air into your bubble. Education and experience will also allow you to build respect from other people for what you are doing and the different goals that you are achieving. Never think that you might be too old to start getting an education of some kind; it's never too late to learn new things, especially when they are new things that will help you to achieve one of your goals. What you learn and experience can often determine your success or failure in life, this is of course obvious. So, make sure you learn to put the right experiences in your bubble, and in turn make your world bigger and better. Just think of all the great achievers there are in the world, some famous ones that we have probably heard of, but actually the majority of these achievers are all kinds of ordinary people that we have never heard of, and that we probably never will hear about either. Anonymous people who have reached their goals in life. Their goals may have been large or small, and their journeys short or long, but they achieved their dreams. They got what they wanted. Some of these people may have achieved a lot, but most people will never know what it is they did, but that doesn't matter because they know what they did, and they savoured the moment of their victory. They were winners and took action to get what they most wanted. Their families must have been very proud of them for what they managed to achieve as well. We all know about the astronaut, or the inventor, or the famous artist, but we don't know about the Mr and Mrs and Miss Smiths' out there – unknown faces, unknown tales of strength, determination, and the sheer will to succeed. These are the people who make up the majority of the goal setters who have put themselves out there and learnt new things and who took action, so that they could say they made it happen and so that they could say that they crossed the finish line for their accomplishments. Now, that's what I call amazing!

"A mind that is stretched by a new experience can
never go back to its old dimensions."
– Oliver Wendell Holmes

CHAPTER 16
Experts/Mentors

If a lack of knowledge is one of the things that is stopping you from proceeding with taking the steps needed to reach your goals, then you need to ask experts within that field of expertise and perhaps even find yourself a mentor. Experts will willingly give you the bits of information that you are seeking. A mentor will not only provide information, they will also be able to guide you through the processes and give you their support whilst also cheering you on. If you can find the expert opinions and guidance of both a mentor and an expert, then although they may vary from one another, they may also lead to good and helpful information, and then you will be onto a winner!

It is not always a good idea, however, to follow too many experts; I have pointed out that opinions can vary, but it is vital that you have these experts anyhow, just pick and choose what information seems to fit best with what you are doing, and if you are still unsure then just research what they have told you. Usually someone gives a piece of advice and it's like: 'Oh, yeah, why didn't I think of that!'

A mentor could be someone you know, or perhaps a person that you have connected with via social media.

Most people who are considered experts within their field of knowledge are pretty good at giving out advice and don't mind you contacting them – obviously, if you are on Twitter or Facebook, for example, then it is polite to like and follow them, and like and share their posts as well. If the person who you have decided you want to seek advice from is very famous, an 'A' lister perhaps, then you are likely going to be disappointed. I am afraid that these people usually only connect with other 'A' listers. If your chosen expert or potential mentor is from the same county as you, or they live local to you, then that's even better; they are much more likely to connect with you. This is not always the case, of course, but you can always try it and see. Sometimes it can take a while to find the right connections, but when you do, it is worthwhile and makes your progress easier and faster, and also gives you a professional's viewpoint. It is, however, always important to get the correct information or else it may hold you up and you may have to start all over again on particular steps on your list. Look on YouTube and you will find a great deal of information on there, and you will also be able to connect with the people in these videos, as they usually leave a link to their website or social media, you can also leave a comment asking a question to do with whatever it is you are looking into and you may well get some very useful answers.

Having an expert, and hopefully a mentor, in your life will make all the difference in your journey to reaching your goals and it will also save you so much time. It can mean the difference between success and failure. After all, these experts have already done what you want to do and are also just the sort of people that you need to be speaking to. So, get messaging, politely of course, and try your luck. If you don't ask, then you don't get. Although don't be disappointed if they don't reply or if they take ages to reply to you, these people tend to be busy most of the time. So, many people are afraid to ask for help, you shouldn't be, some people can be so kind and so helpful, you really will be surprised. There is a whole world of information and help out there, so it is important that you go and find it, pronto! You should never let self-doubt, shyness, lack of confidence, or whatever else it may be stopping you from asking for advice and information, after all what's the worst that could happen? They say no, sorry, I can't help you. That would admittedly be something that you would have to get over and move on from, after all you thought that you had found your ideal expert, but there will also be others who will be more than willing to help you out. I have had a mentor helping me with the whole book writing thing; he's been great, and he is a really kind person. I needed a lot of help starting out as I knew nothing about writing a book and getting it published. I needed a lot of help! One of my goals is to be an author and help other people out there to be able to reach their goals as well, it's been an ambition of mine for a while now, so I decided it was time to take action and start writing. There have been a lot of steps that I've needed to take to complete this book, far more than I initially thought there would be, and having a mentor has been really great, informative and a real eye opener. Information and knowledge are power. Knowledge is your ladder up to the next level of your life and each step up is a step closer to reaching your goals.

There are different kinds of experts and mentors out there. Here are some examples:

- Organisations – contact different organisations in your field of interest for information on the subject you are looking into, and they will put you in touch with helpful professionals.

- Join clubs – for instance you may want to start playing a particular sport, these clubs will help you to develop your skills. There are so many clubs out there, for everything you can think of from A-Z.

- Read books by the experts you want to learn from and those who have already done whatever it is you want to do. You could also subscribe to various magazines which may have useful articles and may also have an advertising page; this could lead you to your expert/mentor and provide you with some great information.

- Re-train to become an expert yourself! Find out what the best courses for you to take would be and why. It is also important to find out any costs and the qualifications you will have when you have completed the training and if it's insurable.

Many successful people who have reached a goal have attributed their success to having a mentor. They have been invaluable in many ways. There are various things a mentor may be able to help with:

- A mentor can provide details relating to their experiences when they were doing something, and how they accomplished their goal.

- Guidance: this is important, because many things that a person may try to do, will often require some form of guidance.

- A mentor will motivate you to carry on and not give up.

- If you're lucky, then a mentor may provide you with emotional support if things go wrong, and also help to set you back on the right path again.

- A mentor can be a role model in your life and will be someone who you look up to.

- They can provide advice that will help you to set the right goals, so that you are more likely to succeed.

- Provide information relating to available resources.

- Pass on useful contacts.

A mentor can be an 'everyday' person that you know. Perhaps it could be a friend or relative, or someone you have been put in touch with through friends because it's someone who has also helped them – they do say that it's who you know, not what you know! Sometimes this is true. Although, of course, it is always best to know what you need to as well. Knowledge combined with the right contacts or mentor is the best possible way to go forward. If you are in the lucky position of already having lots of contacts within the field that your goal is in, then that's great. Most people have contacts of some sort, people that they deal with, perhaps even on a daily basis, for instance if you are a builder you will likely know of lots of contacts within the building industry, that's no surprise. It's when you are looking to do something different from your norm, something outside of your box, that you may find you do not know anyone and will then need to find these experts, and then develop relationships with these people. This will take some time and research, but it's worth the effort, believe me! When you do have these experts, and hopefully a mentor as well, then that it is a definite positive, and you should make the most of it and learn all that you can, and then you will find that the steps towards your goals become easier by far.

"Onwards and upwards."
– C.S. Lewis

CHAPTER 17
The Past – Don't Go There

If you are the sort of person who finds themselves looking back to the past, then you must try to get yourself out of this mindset. You need to be looking forward towards your future and concentrate on your goals. Looking back and re-living your past experiences is rarely a good thing to do, unless the memories you're looking back on are good ones, in which case it's fine to remember these good times with family, friends, on holidays, or whatever else it may be that made you happy back then. If, however, some of your memories are negative ones it is a good idea to consciously try not to think back on them and if that is something you find impossible to do, then it may be best to seek help to deal with whatever it is that is a bad memory from your past. For example, you might have been bullied, threatened, lost someone, or even been abused. Experiences like these need to be faced and dealt with, often with the help of a professional. These types of negative experiences can stop you from moving forward with your life, and may prevent you from doing certain things, including setting and reaching your goals. Hopefully your past experiences were not as negative as the examples given above, but if they were then I would recommend hypnotherapy to help you if you are someone who has found these things hard to forget and recover from. Find a therapist who specialises in whatever it is you need help with.

Of course, there are many other kinds of therapy out there, so find the one that suits you best, if therapy is something that you think you may need. Another thing for you to remember is that nobody is beyond help – nobody at all. I truly believe this. Regardless of what it is that the past held for you, it's time to start visualising the future and what you want it to be, not only in relation to the type of goals, but also how you may want to reinvent yourself, how you will feel and think, what kind of attitude you will have – a positive one, of course! Always strive to think of yourself as a confident person. Begin each day by thinking about the future and seeing in your mind's eye who you will be when you have reached your goal. Everyone's journey is going to be different. We are all unique beings, and our life experiences will be unique to us, however, we can dictate to a large extent how we choose to be from now on. We can all try to shape our futures so that we can achieve better outcomes and experiences.

You need to learn from the past and use it as a way of guiding you so that you know what doesn't work for you anymore or the situations and things that it is probably best you avoid, as well as what lessons the past has taught you. You may feel negative about past events, or maybe even angry; always use your anger and any other negative emotions as a driving force. Flip it over. Use this negative energy and put it into doing positive things and then you will eventually find that you have come out the other side of it better and feeling great and more positive about life. I am not saying that you will forget about the past, but when you have practised positive living for long enough you will start to think differently about your life, your experiences and also the other people who may have played a part in your past. Eventually you may even find that you can look at the past in a different way, a more accepting way. You may even find that you are more understanding about what happened and perhaps even why it happened. This may lead to some kind of closure for you. Coming through the other side of dark periods of your life will, however, take time and a lot of work on yourself.

Forgiveness is also a good thing here, forgive yourself or others for past mistakes; draw a line under each negative experience and move forward. Always move forward, never backwards. If you want to concentrate on your goals then you need to get this sorted out, if it is something that applies to you, because you should only be striving for a better future, not looking back at the past and feeling awful. The past can sometimes stop you from moving forward, do not let it do so! As I've already said, draw a line under it, get some help if you need to, always keep in mind your future goals, and do not live in the past.

So, yes there are many people who will let the past stop them from moving on. They may feel unworthy of happiness and achieving their dreams, and perhaps something may have happened in the past to wipe out their confidence, so for them it may be a case of: "I'm not leaving my box, it's too hard out there, I can't do it." If that rings a bell with you, then you will need to work on yourself first, and you should make this your first goal before anything else that you plan to do. Carefully consider all of the reasons why you may feel like that and analyse it. Write it down and study it. How can you fix things? Fixing it is something you must, and you can do. Push yourself to make the necessary changes required to overcome these kinds of blocks that are a result of past negative experiences. The future doesn't have to be the same way. The future is yet to be written by you. There are always ways to find a solution and resolve any issues, so that you are no longer hung up on the past and whatever it is that happened back then. Only you can make the moves to conquer the blocks that are in your way. No one can do it for you, at the end of the day you need to take responsibility for your own future – and don't we all deserve a great, meaningful, and successful future? We should all have that – no arguments from me there!

The past may have contained such things as being let down; having to be in the company of unpleasant people; being led up the garden path by idiots; being taken advantage of; losing your job; or even being told that you can only do certain types of work because of your sex and background. Actually, with the last example, I was once told by a career's advisor that the career I wanted at the time was probably not a good fit for me, as I didn't have enough qualifications and because a 16-year-old girl would be better off doing an office job typing or working in a shop! I wasn't very impressed. Not that there was anything wrong with those jobs, they were pretty good jobs, it was just that I had set my heart on something else. Something that I had long been thinking about. So, instead of getting any advice or encouragement, or being put in contact with some useful places and people, I was instead given a list of different jobs – typing jobs. Don't get me wrong, at 16 years of age it wasn't all that bad, and in the end, I took the work. At the time attitudes towards females who wanted to step outside of their normal working environment and do something other than cleaning, cooking, factory work, or office work, wasn't thought of in the way that it is now, it was very much a case of girls being considered as only being able to do certain jobs and they weren't allowed to try and get above their station. You were definitely discouraged from doing any types of work that were outside of what was considered the norm, especially if you came from a working-class background. Back then it seemed as though it was okay and completely normal for females to not have any ambitions. It was a different era though; back then attitudes were so entrenched in patriarchy, it was absolutely everywhere, and it was hard to escape it. But that was in the past, things have changed, and still are changing. Now anything is possible.

"The past is a foreign country;
they do things differently there."
– L.P. Hartley

CHAPTER 18
Days Off

Sometimes you might feel under pressure to complete tasks on your lists, do everything in your normal day to day life, fit in family and friends and a social life and perhaps even more on top of that. There may be times, however, where you might be having an off day, or you could be suffering with a health issue, or you may have had a hectic week at work and you just need to catch up on your sleep and chill out, or even just have a bit of time to get over something. This happens to all of us every now and then, it's just part of life. Do not worry if you need to rest up or give yourself a break now and again. It's completely normal and probably a good idea anyway, as it stops burnout. According to research, a Wednesday is actually a good day to take a break because a mid-week break means you won't have as much disruption throughout the rest of the week.

Some people, however, are hell-bent on trying to do everything at once or in a short time frame, and they will often then suffer from burn out. That is obviously never good. Be sure to give yourself regular breaks from the things that are on your lists, so that things are then more spaced out and will fit into your daily and weekly schedules. Trying to cram in more and more things a day, when you have not first reorganised your time-management schedule will not work. That will just put you under more stress instead. There are only a certain number of hours in each day after all! Underestimating completion times could mean that you begin to think about giving up, as you didn't realise it would take so long; don't let this happen. If things take longer than you first thought – and that can happen a lot – then give yourself credit for what you have done so far, but also continue to ensure that you are having regular breaks or days off, and basically pace yourself. Pacing yourself will mean that you are putting yourself under less pressure, and when you are under less pressure mistakes are less likely to happen and you will be better able to deal with everything that has to be done as well. Psychologically, you are then also more likely to carry on with your tasks to completion. Pacing yourself means that you can also ensure you are scheduling time for yourself as well as all the other things that we all find ourselves needing to do, such as shopping, housework, going to work, taking the dog for a walk, spending time with family, or whatever else it may be. So, do not stress, you will achieve what you want, it just needs to be tailored to the time that you have available as well as how you are feeling on that particular day. I am not suggesting that you give up some days just because you cannot be bothered, what I do mean though, is that if you need to rest up, catch up, or do other important jobs then that is what you will need to do. Only you will know what you need to prioritise each day. Then once you have done what it is that you needed to do you will be able to start on your list again and return to doing whatever it is that was put aside. Remember, human beings are not robots; we do need days off now and again.

When you are having some time off from completing your tasks and lists, do not constantly think about what it is that you are not doing or worry that you are missing out or getting behind on the things you would have been doing. Concentrating on the tasks you have yet to do and worrying about them won't get them done any faster and will only serve as a way of further depleting your energy and causing unnecessary frustration. A day off is a day off! Just relax and use the time to re-charge your batteries and get those energy levels back up again. Catch up with some sleep, go for a slow walk, eat healthy foods; it's also a good idea to cut right down on alcohol or even skip it altogether to give your system a rest if you can.

If you want to do something, then maybe just add to your lists and make a note of any tasks that you will need to do when you are back to your normal routine. Always make sure to keep your lists in a safe place, where they are all together and organised so that you know where they are should you need to lay your hands on them quickly. Your lists are private and will probably contain a lot of information about you, your hopes and dreams, your weaknesses and strengths etc, so be careful to keep them safe and perhaps lock them away somewhere, away from prying eyes, dogs and cats who are curious (and very muddy pawed), and children as well – they might decide to use your lists as something for their drawing! Having some quality time to yourself is always a good idea as well because it provides you with the opportunity to reset yourself both mentally and physically. Nothing leads to feeling exhausted more than over working yourself for long periods of time without taking a break. Even having one day off has its benefits. Having a day, or a few days off, helps with many things:

- Helps with your health.

- De-stresses you.

- Lowers anxiety.

- Increases your satisfaction with life in general.

- Helps to increase your productivity when you return to work or doing things towards your goals.

- You are more focused.

- You will enjoy your work more once you get back to your routine.

- Provides you with a better work life balance.

I know that I sometimes need a time out from work and my projects. It's the same for everyone. Getting your work life balance right is so important, and it means that you can then put more energy into something you are working on, when you've had a break and returned to it feeling full of get up and go, and you are also able to look at it with fresh eyes. Sometimes, the break in your work may be because of a delay and you could be waiting for some information, or whatever else it may be, to arrive before you can continue on with things. If that's the case and you can't do anything about it, then just take the opportunity for you to have a relaxing time and switch off. If you are a very driven person, then switching off can be hard, if not impossible for some people; there are, however, various things you can try to help you relax. Try yoga, meditation, or listening to some relaxing music, go for a walk out in nature, or whatever it may be that will work for you to help you wind down for a little while. Also, it's sometimes a good idea to try unplugging devices and having less screen time, reading a good book for instance and also make sure that your home environment is a tranquil and peaceful space where you are able to chill out.

Whatever kind of day off you are having just be kind to yourself, chill out and relax; remember your lists and tasks will still be there when you return.

"Rest and be thankful."
– William Wordsworth

CHAPTER 19
Support

If you have no support around you, then you need to get some. If you do have great support, then that's going to be a big help to you. Getting the right kind of support is an ideal thing to have as you will feel more motivated and it will make completing your steps easier and you will, of course, feel more confident as well. Always try to surround yourself with people who are on your side and support what it is you are doing. Real friends will always do this anyway and will give you their full support, but there will also always be those who will doubt you and think that you are ridiculous for even trying to achieve your goal and will try to drag you down. They usually make negative comments and generally have a negative attitude. The critical doubters will always want to bring you down to their level – so do not allow yourself to go there!

You deserve your dream, and no-one has the right to diminish that in any way. It could be that someone close to you is just concerned or worried that you might fail and end up disappointed and that you will have wasted your time and efforts. It is understandable for family and partners to want to shield you from any disappointments, you just need to talk to them about what you want to do and explain all the ins and outs of it. They will come to realise that you are serious and that you really are determined and then they will support you going forward. Fake friends and acquaintances who put you down and gossip about you wanting to do something with your life – you do not need that! Just ignore these people. I am not suggesting that you be rude, but maybe that you understand that not everyone will be pleased for you and support your ideas. That is okay, just find the people who do.

Some years ago, I had a good friend who wanted to go to a particular music concert. She had told her friends and they just laughed about it because they liked a different kind of music altogether. They did not think she was serious about it at all. The concert tickets were very expensive, and my friend was just doing temp work at the time so she could not really afford to buy the ticket and pay for travel to the concert. So, she began a plan of action which would lead to her making more money each week. Basically, she got more work cleaning over a couple of her days off and doing some bar work clearing tables on the days she couldn't find cleaning work. The work was not what she had trained for nor was it what she wanted to be doing, but she stuck to her plan and saved up the money that she needed to be able to go to the concert. She told her friends about all of this and their response was less than supportive; in fact, they seemed jealous about it. She went to the concert anyway, and she had a great time; it was a dream come true – one of them anyway.

My friend has now found new friends, including me, who are always pleased when she gets to do something that she wants to do. I always cheer my friends on whenever they achieve anything. But as you can see, not everyone does. So, find the right kind of friends, experts, mentors, or whoever it may be to support you in reaching each of your goals, it makes the whole journey much easier and it makes for a much more comfortable ride altogether.

Being able to talk to your family about taking each step will also help you feel more confident about the whole thing and hopefully you will have a family support system that you can rely on and trust to always be there for you whatever happens in life's ups and downs.

- Surround yourself with positive people.

- Expect critics when you want to do something out of the norm, but if you have a good support network around you, then any negativity won't matter.

- Tell those closest to you about your goals – get their support.

- Give yourself as much kindness and support as you can – you know you deserve it.

- If you need extra support, find it.

Your ideas, and I'm sure you have a lot of them, need a solid base of support. You will also be more likely to succeed if you never let others down and always finish whatever you start. Always be the sort of person who finishes a project; that way you keep your word to yourself as well as your word to others. You may also need additional support when the going gets tough, and if the people around you are not interested in your goals then you will have to look elsewhere for that support. It can sometimes be the case that those who are closest to us are not actually all that interested in the things that we are planning. Instead share your ideas with someone who has already done similar and who is also someone you admire, this keeps you on your toes and makes you more motivated to continue with whatever it is you are trying to achieve. This can be because you don't want that person who you look up to, to think less of you, so you will then try even harder to succeed. Telling someone higher up that ladder than you what your goals and ambitions are is a great way to motivate yourself and also helps to keep you on track, and it will also help to keep your ambitions as one of the most important thoughts in your mind. Exciting times for you! You will be more determined to see through your plans if you've told someone who is also a role model to you, rather than if you have only told family and friends. Don't underestimate this approach, as you will need to bolster your resolve from time to time, and these kinds of people will keep you pointed in the right direction, especially when you might be feeling lost or confused in some way.

Pushing on with your goals gives you a sense of pride, self-worth, belonging to something greater than yourself, and will also make you feel more secure about the future. So, as I have said before, getting yourself a mentor to help provide that extra support will be a massive positive. Your journey will be a whole lot easier for you than if you were to try and do everything yourself from scratch and had to figure out all of the ins and outs of the different steps that you would need to take on your own. Okay, yes, you could sort it all out on your own, but then it is also going to take you a lot longer to figure out everything than would be the case if you were to have the support of a mentor. If that's how you want to approach the tasks on your lists, then of course that's fine, that can be only your decision to make at the end of the day – but why would you decide to do that when there is loads of really good help and advice out there just waiting to be discovered by you.

So, support from family and friends is good, support from a mentor is great, but there is also the kind of support that is needed that can only come from you. Whatever kinds of goals you may have, you must consider supporting yourself throughout it all. Be kind to yourself. Rest. Play. Support and love yourself. Self-support is so important, I don't think people realise this sometimes when they are trying to accomplish more in life, that it's all too easy to put every ounce of effort into a project, but that may be to the detriment of your own health and rest, and also can result in spending less time with those you love. Realise that you have to find the right balance and the right support, and that it should start with you supporting yourself.

"The potential for greatness lives within each of us."
– Wilma Rudolph

CHAPTER 20
Fake it Until it's Real

There will be many times in your life where you perhaps do not feel confident, most of us experience this at some point; for others it is a constant issue in their lives, one that they wish they could overcome. If you are in any situation that makes you shake inside, makes you nervous, gives you a sense of dread, or you go blank when you previously knew just what it was that you wanted to say, then please don't despair. There are ways to quickly pull yourself back into a more confident state of mind once again.

What has all this got to do with goal setting and achieving what is rightfully yours? Well, as I have already said in this book, confidence is very important. It may well apply to you reaching your goal more easily as well, and if you lack confidence then it could well stop your progress. Of course, your goal may not be dependent on you having a confident persona – or lack of one. If this is the case, carry on, but it is always good for you to have a degree of confidence, regardless. So, what should you do if you do need to become more confident?

You could always see a therapist of some kind who will be able to help you in becoming a more confident person, and to explore the reasons behind why you are feeling that way, but what do you do in the meantime? Okay, so you fake it. Whilst the therapy process is working to help change your mindset which depending on your individual needs this could well take some time, so here are some things for you to start trying now.

- Look in the mirror every morning and say nice things to yourself – you love yourself, right? You're as good as anyone else and you need to remind yourself of that.

- Stand up straight, do not slouch, not even when you are sitting down, sit with a straight back. It does not matter if you relax and slouch on your sofa at night; you are at home, but when you are with other people you need to come across as someone who is confident. Standing up tall and straight immediately makes you look more confident and even makes you look younger. Practice it in the mirror – do you see a difference?

- Speak your affirmations before you leave the house everyday – don't ever say negative words to yourself, instead only say positive words to yourself.

- Model yourself on someone who you admire, who is also a good role model and someone very confident.

- Smile – this is so important as you need to convey a good outgoing image. Do not look miserable, people do not want to do business or connect with a sad, miserable person; that is human nature. People will want to connect with someone who is positive. If you are feeling sad about something then find help of some sort, and in the meantime, fake it. Sometimes you need to smile even when you don't really feel like doing so. There is research that says smiling more sends positive messages to the brain, it tricks the brain into believing that you are actually happy, even when you may not be! Over time you will actually become less sad and instead find yourself becoming happier. Have you ever noticed how successful people are always smiling and laughing? Try smiling more and see if it works for you and makes some difference.

- If you act confidently over a long period of time, then you are more likely to actually become a more confident person. It becomes a habit. Eventually, when you have added in more experiences and learnt that you shouldn't care so much about what others think of you, it will mean that you have become more confident anyway.

- Never respond to a person negatively. People do not like it and it could end up making a situation worse. If a friend's going through a hard time, give them positive responses like: 'I'm sure things will turn around for you soon, you'll be back up there again and better than ever.' Do not start moaning and whingeing about your problems either, always be the positive and confident one. I know that this can be hard at times, we all have days when nothing is really going to plan, but if you want to be a confident person then you first have to learn to respond in a positive way to any problems that may arise. Being positive also causes you less stress as well.

- Be around people who want to help you, people who are on your side, this will add to your confidence massively.

- Eye contact – maintain eye contact but don't stare.

- Watch your body language – it can giveaway your inner emotions.

- Breathe! A lot of nervous and unconfident people have shallow breathing.

- Don't mumble or stumble over your words. Slow down your speech and be sure to articulate precisely.

I would also add that if you are faking confidence and have decided not to address the issues that are causing your lack of confidence, either with a therapist or through some other means, then probably you won't be able to keep faking it up for long. It is a pretence after all. You may start to put yourself under pressure and you will be concentrating so much on the things that you need to do to come across as this super confident person, that you will begin to make "mistakes" relating to things such as your body language, speech, your mind starting to go blank etc; you are basically regressing back to your usual self again. So, faking it might be okay for a quick meeting, or a few phone calls, but anything longer than this might result in you beginning to struggle with those same old patterns emerging once more. If you are naturally a quiet person then it's not likely that you'll become a party animal anytime soon! So, what! It's more important to be the real you and learn to be confident in your own abilities so that you are able to get out there and begin on the road to the wonderful goals that you have set yourself. Forget fitting in with what other people think you should be like. Trying to meet other people's expectations will cause you to become more unconfident if you keep failing to meet those expectations time and time again. So, don't try. As soon as you stop trying to be something that you're not, the whole thing becomes easier for you because the pressure is off. When you are the more authentic version of yourself, and you have started doing a lot more things in your life; adding in experiences and achieving your goals, then this will lead to you being more confident anyway. The validation of others becomes less important. I'm not saying that we all shouldn't care about what others think of us, after all we do all want to be liked and appreciated, and that's a good thing. As I have said previously, having positive people around you who believe in you and what you are trying to achieve can massively help to improve your confidence, in leaps and bounds in fact! But what happens when they are not around, and you then have to rely on your own get up and go? Will that get up and go then disappear? So, if confidence to get out there and achieve things is going to be a problem for you, then I would say to get some help with it or expect it to take a longer time to overcome on your own – which is one reason why you may want to fake it until you can make it real and overcome that lack of confidence, and in the meantime, you can use some of these tricks to help you get by. The older you get the more confident you will eventually become anyway, as you will have had many years where you will have been experiencing different things, and you will have met a lot of different people and have gone through a lot in your life. People can change, and people do change all of the time, to then become a more improved version of themselves. If more confidence is what you need, then you can get it, it is possible, don't think that it's not. Indeed, being more confident may in fact be one of your goals.

"Nothing great was ever achieved without enthusiasm."
– Ralph Waldo Emerson

CHAPTER 21
Bridge to Happiness

Everyone has to build a bridge. This is of course a metaphorical bridge, and you have to ask yourself how you are going to build it, and what materials you will need. Your bridge represents your journey to meet your goals and also how you will go about achieving that and what practical steps are needed to build the bridge. What knowledge will you need, what costs are involved, how long will it take? Each piece of your bridge will have to be put together one brick at a time. Ask yourself, what will your bridge look like, what type of bridge is it, and how will you cross it, and what will you find on the other side? Your bridge to success enables you to get from where you are now, to crossing over to your end goal on the other side. As you build up your steps, and put in place each thing on your lists you need to do, you then build each piece of your bridge. You will have to make the bridge very strong so you can cross it with ease. If you don't know how to start with the whole bridge building enterprise, then of course you begin with getting the right materials needed to make a proper job of it, and the right expertise so you know how to go about putting it all together. Some people's bridges are made of bricks, or stone and iron, and others are simple wooden bridges; which are built a lot quicker, and require a bit less effort. Whatever type it is you will need to put it all together so it all fits properly and is very secure. This will then mean you are able to cross it and have confidence that you will reach the other side. When you get to the other side, enjoy what's waiting there for you after all your hard work. If you are reaching your goals and it is not making you feel really great, really happy, and giving you a sense of pride then something is not right. If you ever take notice of someone who is successful in some way, maybe through their business or through life in general, then it's an odds-on certainty that they are working hard to build their own bridge and are enjoying what they find when they cross over that bridge. Their demeanour also generally seems to be very upbeat and happy – pretty happy in fact! Of course it does – they have just built this fantastic structure and achieved their dream.

So you should be enjoying your successes and goals as well as also ensuring you enjoy the general bridge building experience. If you reach a goal and you are feeling deflated; or let down in some way; or a little bit flat, then maybe that goal is not really what you should have been aiming for. Maybe your perceived goal was only what you thought you should have been doing, not what you actually want to be doing. If this is the case, then re-work your lists to better suit you.

Your bridge should also have some strong foundations so that it is able to withstand any setbacks that you may face along the way. Get those foundations right and then everything else should be easier to build upon and it should also be easier for you to be able to continue expanding towards your chosen goal. If you do not get the foundation work right, then the foundations will begin to crumble away if any pressure is put on them, say, from things that you have not yet learnt to do properly or from steps you forgot to do. Bridges are put together piece by piece, and you must put together all of the pieces you need, not only to form a strong foundation of knowledge, but to love what you are doing at each stage of the journey on the way towards your dreams. Building bridges is exciting! As you are getting somewhere you want to be.

I have met some people who did not enjoy the process of reaching a goal and felt let down when they did reach the goal; it was not what they expected to find at the end of their rainbow, and for them it felt like a waste of precious time and energy. Make sure, before you start your lists, that your goal really is what you want to be doing and that it will fit in with your current lifestyle and also the lifestyles of those around you who you may want help from with certain tasks.

Always have a good think before you begin each goal and if you do need to adjust your lifestyle, plan how you are going to be able to do that. On a scale on one to ten, one being the easiest and ten being the hardest: how easy is it going to be? There are usually ways around certain blocks that may be in the way of your goals, that you will be able to overcome, even if there does not seem to be a way around it and you have racked your brain for the answers. Consult an expert in the field that you are interested in and see how they did it or get advice from their point of view based on your circumstances. Asking someone else for an opinion is free and it is also good to see things from another person's perspective. They could come up with all sorts of things that may have never occurred to you. Of course, you must first make sure that you ask the right people, this is not always easy to judge.

In the past I have asked certain people for advice on different subjects and they were no help at all! In fact, they obviously just couldn't be bothered to help. Speaking to people like this who have a slightly negative outlook on life will not be helpful at all. Instead, just thank them and move on to the next person on your list of contacts. Do not linger on the words of someone who was no help. Maybe they were having an off day, maybe they just did not know anything about it, or maybe they could not be bothered to help you! Either way – next!

Building your bridge to success may take a very long time indeed, depending on your circumstances. Other people who have done what you want to do may have done it fairly quickly. Although they perhaps had plenty of time and money, the right connections, maybe they already had the necessary expertise to do it, therefore making it easier for them to complete their goal quickly. That was their journey and their circumstances, do not think that you have to achieve your goals in the same time frame as someone else; your lists and goals must be tailored to you alone and your particular timetable, based on your level of experience, time availability, money, health and a hundred and one other things that may come into play.

But maybe the problem or obstacle to your progress is that your significant other has a problem with you stepping outside of your usual box. This can happen and end your bridge building. A few years ago, I attended an interview with an insurance company. I thought that it was what I wanted to do at the time, and I also thought I would be able to make more money doing insurance work, rather than what I was doing then. I was ushered into this man's office for the interview, and when I sat down the interviewer began to ask me questions about my family life. I thought to myself, what has that got to do with anything? He then went on to say that their job vacancy arose because the last person who worked there had left due to a family problem. Apparently, what had happened was that the lady had worked for them for about a year and she became very successful within the insurance company and had earned great commission, approximately £60,000. Okay, I thought, not bad. The interviewer then went on to tell me that the lady's husband was not supportive of her career at all. In fact, he resented the fact that she was earning more money than him. So, this lady then reluctantly decided to save her marriage and instead leave her job at the insurance company. It was a great pity; she had loved her job, but her husband was not having any of it. He was not very supportive, so what this tells us is that it is vital that your other half – if you have one – is onboard with your plans otherwise you could encounter problems during your bridge building.

Your partner needs to be a part of your support network. Speak to them about your goal, gauge their response, ask them what they think about it, ask if they will help you and support you. Discuss it with them often so that they know what is going on and will become used to the idea of you wanting to, for example: train to climb Kilimanjaro, or whatever else it is that your goal might be. Maybe they would like to accompany you on this journey. Hopefully, a partner will be cooperative and pleased that you are doing something that you have always wanted to do. They should support you, not knock you down. If you are reluctant to speak to your partner, then are you possibly afraid that they will laugh at you, ridicule you, or not take your idea seriously? This indicates that there is something wrong and you need to find out what it is and address that. Will your partner or friends change their opinion when they see that you are serious about achieving your goal? Perhaps not, some people feel threatened by others wanting to do things, things that might lead to them becoming more successful, more powerful, richer, or even happier.

Do discuss it at length so they understand more about it. Either way, do try to sort it out otherwise you may find that you begin to feel stuck and unable to move forward. That is the worst-case scenario though. In the majority of cases husbands, wives, partners, or best friends will support you. Whoever it is that is closest to you in life, they should be your number one cheerleader willing you on to reach the finish line – which is the other side of the bridge.

"Discipline is the bridge between goals and accomplishment."
– Mother Teresa

CHAPTER 22
Trip to Willingsville

Take a trip to Willingsville then make sure to travel on to your first stop at Action Town. It will be fun; you'll like it there and you may even get to see Dream City. Obviously, by this I mean that you have to do the work and take the actions that are needed in order to reach your goals. You need to be willing to put the work in and take the actions necessary so that they will lead you to fulfilling your goals and dreams! Simple. You have to really want it. There are lots of people out there who are not really willing to put themselves out there and step outside of the box they have put themselves in, or even the box that other people have put them in. This is one of the main reasons that will contribute to their goals not being achieved and their dreams not coming true. If you want to live that dream, then you are going to have to fight for it and overcome any obstacles that you may need to in order to reach that goal or dream. If you're not willing to take a risk and leave your box and take these massive actions, then it's unlikely that you'll get very far in achieving your goals. This would be a shame and a waste of your talents and potential.

If you are not willing to take steps towards a goal, then you might end up with regrets one day – regrets that you haven't done anything when you actually had the chance to go for it. This is what happened to someone I once knew. She had ambitions, actually she had lots of them. She was an office clerk, and a good one at that, she worked hard and was well liked by all who knew her. Although there wasn't much variation in her day-to-day life – she went to work, cooked dinner when she got home, watched tv, brushed her teeth and went to bed and that was pretty much it, except for on the weekends when she would visit her family and friends. She commuted to work by train every day and her journey was fairly predictable and lacked any real excitement. The one thing that drew her interest was the beautiful scenery that she would admire on her daily train journeys. She longed for the great outdoors. This lady had a dream to be free of the 9 to 5 office life. She wanted to work within the agricultural industry in some way or another – to be surrounded by the green landscapes; to care for animals; to breathe in the fresh country air. She would look at the fields and hedgerows and trees, as she passed by them on the train and would think to herself: 'I wonder who lives and works there, I wish it was me.' She already owned a house in a city, one which she could have sold so that she would've been able to move to the country and purchase a small holding. It would have been exactly what she had always wanted to do. Except she couldn't bring herself to take that chance, to leave her box and follow her dream. She was accustomed to her life in the city, she didn't know anything else. So, instead of researching her options and looking into training and small holding courses, she decided that where she already was in life was the only option for her. In her eyes, it was for the best and it wasn't something that could be changed – how could it right? I mean she had to make the train on time for work because her colleagues would be expecting her, and who would there be to do all the filing and make coffee for the boss. It would be a disaster if she wasn't there! Of course, all these excuses were just a cop out. She wasn't willing to make the changes that would be needed to get what it was that she thought she wanted. I say what she thought she wanted, as she didn't really want it did she? She was happy to stay in her box and not take a chance. It was comfortable there, and familiar. As far as I know, she's still working in that same office, still doing the same job, and still gazing out the window of the train as the green countryside passes her by.

Often times the box that you are in, or the category that you find yourself labelled under – usually by other people and their opinions and expectations of you – might make you feel that your only option is to remain there, stuck in the box that you have been hiding in and that you have been too afraid to come out of, as was the case in the example above. But instead look around you and hold your head up high and say to the world: 'Hi, it's me. Here I am, I'm going to live my life my way from now on.' That is what you need to be doing. The people around you will either be able to deal with the new you or maybe they will not. If they do not like that you are stepping outside of your 'box', venturing out into the world, setting goals and taking actions, and having your own dreams, then so be it, that's not your problem is it? That is their choice, not yours. Just carry on, after all you only get one life, and that life is too short for you to waste it not doing the things that you want to be doing for yourself. Our beliefs shape our reality, and you need to believe that you can do the things that you want to achieve, and that means rising above any self-doubt.

You need to be willing to start making the necessary changes within your life and to also take daily action towards your goals, and actually start living your dreams. At the beginning this may well be a hard thing for you to do, but it does get easier and easier as you make more progress towards your goals and dreams. You just have to change your mindset and get yourself some grit and determination, start planning and writing those lists, and when you do this that will then mean that you will find reaching your goals that much easier, and they will seem like a much more real possibility and then you will reach your final destination of Successville.

"The journey of a thousand miles begins with a single step."
– Lao Tzu

CHAPTER 23

Comfort Zone or Twilight Zone?

Comfort Zone

This is your known area; it is easy for you to just stay there because it is a safe place where nothing much changes for you. It is the place where you are used to being and it feels familiar and comfortable to you. You are used to the way things have been for so long that it has become a daily routine and a habit to just carry on as you are. You will need to get out of your comfort zone at some point if you want to move forwards with your steps to reach your goals, there is no way of escaping it.

Many find this to be a daunting thing to do, it is scary, it is the unknown, it is like the Twilight Zone. Yes, okay, it can feel that way because it is a different experience and level of being. When you do something that you are not used to then it will feel strange and maybe even a little bit scary, but sometimes you have to push yourself outside of your zone of comforts in order for you to be able to realise the goals and dreams that you may want to achieve for yourself. A certain degree of courage will be needed here. The reason, or one of the main reasons, why a person does not achieve their goals is because they are reluctant to try and do something different or to experience new things, because it is too scary, new, different, challenging or any one of the many other emotions that could be connected to this. That is a normal reaction that anyone is likely to get from sticking their head up out of the box that they have been living in and then seeing the unfamiliar that is all around them. Get used to this idea. This is what it will take. Anyone who has achieved amazing things has had to do it, if they hadn't then they wouldn't have got very far at all. All professionals, high earners, business owners, sports people, inventors, entrepreneurs, or anyone else who has been successful in some way, has had to acquire some grit and just go for it. Comfort Zone. Nah!

When I decided to retrain as a hypnotherapist and holistic therapist, it wasn't easy for me; I had to save up the money for the courses as well as everything else that was involved in order for me to be able to set up a practice. I also needed to overcome any shyness and lack of confidence – yes, really! All therapists have something that they will likely need to sort out and overcome in their lives in order to get to where they want to be, just like anyone else. I did what I had to, and I succeeded. The training I did gave me the confidence to start my own business and it is the best thing I have ever done, but in order to do that I have had to put myself out there and accept that some people will be pleased for me and cheer me on – go for it! – and some may not have been quite so happy for me, as I had stepped out of my box and done something really different from what I was doing before and that would have come as a surprise to some people. That is just life, you cannot care about what people say or think about you if you want to get on and succeed. It is a big world out there, it is not just the small piece of it that you already know all too well, so go and do what you need to do in order to succeed. Repeatedly stepping out of your comfort zone will accustom you to different experiences and how those experiences will feel for you, so do it often and you will find it easier to do whatever it is that you want to. It becomes familiar and then it doesn't scare you quite so much anymore; you have learnt that it is okay for you to do these new things and it was actually easier than you thought it would be. Hesitation and procrastination can kill your dreams, so you should try not to indulge in those things. Decide what it is that you want and how you will get it, and then take constant action until you have completed each step.

Twilight Zone

The Twilight Zone is probably what it will feel like when you first start doing tasks that you are not used to. Scary, unfamiliar, other-worldly, uncomfortable, strange and just downright awkward at times! But as long as you know what it is that you are doing, what you are aiming for and you have done your research and checked with a doctor if necessary and applicable – if you goal involves exercise that you are not used to doing (see the 'Safety First' chapter) – and you have also made your lists before starting your project or task, then it should inspire you and it will also be easier for you to make a start. Taking small steps towards your goal will also have the added benefit of you becoming more used to doing things that are outside of your normal routine. Your confidence will grow as you progress towards your goals. Face your fears and up your game, then get out there and make it happen. You must have faith in yourself.

It might be that you want to join a gym, but you feel that you are too overweight to go and exercise around the fit and skinny people who will most likely be there. Take it in small steps; check out the gym online, phone up and find out how much a membership is, go there and just take a look around. When you have completed these steps, it will then seem much easier for you to actually join the gym and get fitter with the help of the instructors and trainers there. You can see how I have broken down this task for someone who wants to join the gym but is also hesitant to do so; it can seem daunting for some people, but it may also be a necessary step to take in order to reach your goal, if your goal is something like losing weight or getting fitter, in this case. Someone who is very unfit and overweight and maybe even lacking in confidence, would possibly laugh at you or look absolutely horrified if you were to suggest that they join the gym. 'Me? No way!' That is their point of view from the comfort zone that they are in. To change this perspective, they will first have to venture out into the Twilight Zone of the unknown world, little by little, step by step, until it is no longer scary at all.

"If you do what you've always done, you'll
get what you've always gotten."
– Tony Robbins

CHAPTER 24
Laying Your Strong Foundation

Now that you have read about how you can reach you goals more quickly and you have also read about some therapies that may be able to help you get past any blocks or bad habits that you want to change, in turn enabling you to move forward and maintain your progress and momentum towards your goals, it is now time for you to start taking action!

If you follow some of the suggestions that are in this book then you will hopefully soon begin to see some of the benefits, whether it will take you a short time or a long time to reach your goal, the important thing for you to remember is to never give up. Keep learning, keep planning, keep making those lists, keep positive and keep moving forwards! Do what you need to do, so that you are able to keep achieving those results. It's also advisable to not give yourself impossible goals when you are starting out, start small and build up to the bigger steps and goals. For instance, you might be a couch potato, a very nice one I am sure – who has decided that you want to climb Everest. That is going to be pretty much impossible for a while. I do not say that it is totally impossible, as I'm sure there must be mountain climbers out there who were fairly unfit at one point in their lives, but they started off small and over the years of becoming fitter and healthier, learning the ropes (if you will pardon the pun!) and connecting with the right experts, they then learnt to become mountain climbers. But Everest! It takes the best of the best to even think about doing something like that. So, try and be realistic.

There are many people out there who have achieved the impossible, but it is always best to start off with very small steps and build up to your goal. If you fail, then just start over again and keep plugging away at it until you succeed. Depending on what their aim is, it can sometimes take years for successful people to reach their goals. They just have the right mindset to help them to keep going and giving up is something that never enters their thoughts. They learn from any failures they have experienced; they learn what works and what does not and then they simply adjust their approach. Once you have achieved several small, or medium, steps on the way to your main goal or dream, you will find that what you are doing is laying a foundation for a successful outcome. You will need this foundation otherwise things may not work out and they may fall apart, or you may even think that you have failed before you've begun. Get the foundation for your goals and dreams right and all else will follow suit.

When the Egyptians built the pyramids, they spent a lot of time and effort planning and building the foundation structures that they needed to ensure they were just right so that they could be sure that the rest of the pyramid would stay in place and would not fall down. You can see how important it is to get the basics right. When laying a strong foundation, you have to bear in mind various things, such as INSTINCT. Ask yourself what your instinct tells you about your goals, and about how you will go about completing them. It's also important that you apply your instinct in relation to the people you are involved with in connection to your goal journey; to see how those people fit in, how well they are going to support you, and how good a job they are going to do for you, and of course to see what it is that your instinct tells you about how much you can trust them. This is important, as your instinct will tell you a lot about a situation or person. I know I myself have forgotten to listen to my instinct in the past, and I have lived to regret it. I realised that I should have listened to the little voice inside my head, or gut, telling me that something was not right. My instinct rarely lets me down, so I should have listened to it, however, on that occasion I didn't because I was in a hurry to get something done and went ahead with a step on my list involving a particular company who ended up letting me down and of course a lot of time was then wasted! All because I didn't listen to my instincts, which were telling me that this particular company wasn't the right kind of contact for me to be working with. Most people's instincts are the same, they are pretty reliable; however, it can also be easy for folks to not listen to it because they want things done there and then, they want them done quickly and so they rush into something that isn't right. They were eager to complete something and didn't listen to their inner voice that was telling them that something was wrong with the situation, or person, they had given their trust to. When you do not listen to that inner voice, nine times out of ten you will live to regret it. This will then result in a hold up with your plans or could even put an end to that aspect of your plans altogether. So, it's vital for you to use your instincts as part of your foundation building process. Here is a list of other things you will need as part of your foundation:

- Authenticity
- Courage
- Creativity
- Purpose

- Curiosity
- Passion
- Good values
- Strength of focus
- Faith
- Self-compassion
- Define your weaknesses and overcome them, or work with them.
- Define what your challenges will be.
- Be honest with yourself – what is achievable when starting out?

All of the things listed above should form a part of the foundation to your success for any goals that you may aim for. Big or small. You must also challenge yourself to identify what kind of changes you want to see in your life, and how those changes will help you reach any goals that you are wanting to achieve. It is also important to identify your main strengths. These should be listed in your main lists anyway. So, go back and examine what you have written. These strengths are the things you are best at, and hopefully will be the things that will help you to reach your goals, because focusing on and using these strengths will bring you the best possible benefits and make it easier for you to complete each step or even reach your main goal, if it's something that can be used towards your goal that is. If your strengths lay in other areas that have nothing to do with your ambition, for say starting a business, then you are going to have to learn about those things and create a new set of skills for yourself. This may well become one of your goals on the road to creating a new future. Whatever you do, you first need to be making sure that you get those foundations right, and then you won't go far wrong.

"The man who removes a mountain begins
by carrying away small stones."
– William Faulkner

CHAPTER 25
Do's and Don'ts

This chapter lists various points that are worth bearing in mind when you are striving to meet your dreams and goals. I hope that you will follow most, if not all, of these guidelines as they make achieving your goals much easier, a lot less stressful and will create a more distinct road map for you to follow on your journey to achieving those all-important dreams and goals.

Do's

- Create as detailed a plan as is possible.
- Start with the small steps.
- Write it down; this will make your plans feel more real.
- Be exact about what it is you want.
- Allow for failures; they happen.
- Always keep track of your progress and give yourself credit when reaching each stage of the process.
- Reward any successes that you have – perhaps a meal out to celebrate?
- Do be sure to find yourself a support network.
- Make a commitment to your plan and then stick to it.
- Do take full responsibility for your plans and any changes

you may decide to make.

- Do be brave – leave your box!
- Do always bear in mind safety – always!
- Visualise your goals every day.
- Do take advice from experts.
- Do try and find yourself a mentor.
- Do ensure that you build your lists, the more information you have written down the better.
- Do create a good foundation of skills and/or knowledge before you try to move on to the bigger steps.
- Do be patient.
- Be professional.
- Always keep smiling.
- Do try to make sure that you work within your energy levels, as pushing yourself outside of these energy levels will mean that you may become too tired to continue and your concentration, in turn, will let you down, then mistakes are more likely to be made, so always try and rest when you need to rest.

Don'ts

- Don't wait – someday nearly always means never.
- Don't focus on too many ideas at once. Pick the smallest goals and complete those first.
- Don't forget to give yourself a deadline if possible and applicable, and then try to stick to it.
- Don't reach for 100% if you are only able to give 50% at that time. Remember to work on resting when you need to.
- Don't be a perfectionist.
- Don't talk, or think, yourself into failure. Negative thinking will not help you to reach your goals and dreams.
- Don't get upset if you fail, try again, then again and again.
- Don't ever think that you're not capable of reaching your goals.
- Don't be impatient.
- Don't get angry or sad if you can't do something – instead try and learn how to do it, even if it takes you a while to master a particular task.

- Don't take advice from those people who are not supportive of you, or those who aren't on the same wavelength as you – it's also worth remembering that experts should encourage you if they think that you can go ahead with something.

- Don't give up on a commitment, see it through; be as good as your word.

- Don't get mad at yourself if you cannot meet a deadline. Refresh your deadline and keep going.

- Don't take unnecessary risks, do your research and think everything through carefully.

- Don't take someone else's ideas at face value; look into them carefully and then decide if those ideas are suitable for you and fit in with your own circumstances.

- Don't be a pushover.

- Don't give up on your dreams.

- Don't forget your family and friends; how will your plans affect them?

I hope that some, if not all, of these points will help to guide you on your journey to Successville.

"Do not let others define you, define yourself."
– Ginni Rometty

CHAPTER 26
Reaching Your Goal

Congratulations! You have now reached one of your goals, or perhaps you only had one main goal to begin with. You should feel great and be basking in your success. Reaching a goal and having taken all of the necessary steps in the process – micro-steps and main steps – is fantastic, well done you! You have followed your lists and it has worked. Well, hopefully it has worked if you have done it all correctly, so I trust that it has worked for you. Some of the people who follow goal setting are in what I like to call the 1% club; these are the special few who choose to review their lists, and work on those lists, every day. If you have achieved you goal by using this method and working on your lists every day, then you too are in the 1% club. The 3% club is another great club for you to belong to as well. As you will see in the chapter after this one, where you will learn more about the meanings of these percentages.

Now that you have reached your goal, say it is weight loss and you have now become fitter and healthier in the process; what else is there that needs to be done now that you are where you wanted to be? Well, now that the process has worked for you please remember to not throw away your lists, not one of them, even those lists that didn't work. With some goals it is a possibility that once you have completed them you may then fall back into old patterns and habits and revert to where you were when you started. I am sure you won't let that happen, will you? But it can happen especially with things like weight loss, getting fitter, stopping smoking, and other habit and health-based issues that you may have sorted out for the moment. You really have to be determined and persistent in maintaining these kinds of goals. They are lifelong goals, not just reach my ideal weight and then relax and go back to cheating on your diet. The pounds will just pile on again. You will feel awful and then you will have to start all over again with the very same goal, and then it's back to the lists! It is always best to keep all of your lists and research, contact lists etc, so if you ever do need to start something over again, then you will have it all there ready to go.

A few years ago, when I was a little bit overweight, I decided to start a diet and begin exercising. I had it all planned out: the correct foods to eat, foods to avoid, cooking schedules – my partner wasn't on a diet, so I sometimes cooked different things for him, although he sometimes enjoyed some of the healthy cooking that was going on. I also put an exercise schedule together of certain types of exercises; going for walks or jogs formed a large part of that schedule, although I also included some resistance exercises and Pilates each day as well, and I planned to do so every day, without fail, come rain or shine.

After a few months I had lost all of the weight that I had wanted to lose in order to reach my ideal weight again, but after a while I started to eat out more. It began when we went on holiday and then it just continued after I got home. Slowly I began to put on the weight that I had lost. So, I went back to my lists and schedules and did it all over again. I should never have allowed that weight to creep back on again, and after all that hard work too! I should have known better really, but when you are relaxing and enjoying yourself it is easy to think - okay, I'll have that cake, or I'll have that toasted sandwich! I'm not saying I never have any treats, I am only human after all, but if I ever need to lose a few pounds I now know what works for me and what doesn't, and I just have to re-do the things on my list –

easy, well mostly easy; losing weight and denying yourself all of those nice sweet things can be hard to do at times and it can sometimes be really hard, but like anything that is worth doing you just need to dig deep, be determined, and make it happen one step at a time.

Sometimes it may not have been possible for you to reach a goal; you tried and for whatever reason it just did not work out, or it was plain impossible. You should still give yourself a pat on the back for trying, and for doing your best to reach whatever type of ambition or goal you were aiming for. Then revise your plans and instead try to look at it from a different angle and try to find a way around what it was that blocked you the last time. Basically, regroup and try again and again until you have the solutions, this is something you will have to do if you have your heart set on something that you want to achieve.

Many people do not actually try to reach their goals, or perhaps they will only try for a short time before they give up. By reading this book you have shown that you want to reach your goals and you are prepared to start taking the right actions to get there, which is great. Although I am in no way saying that just by reading this book your life will change for the better overnight, or that you will be able to reach your goals really easily. What it could do, however, is give you helpful ideas and methods that can give you an idea as to how you might get to where you need to be in order to move forward with your plans. Nothing is guaranteed, no-one can guarantee a successful outcome no matter what advice or system it is that you choose to follow, it would be nice if you could. All you can do is try out some of the things that I have written about in this book and do your level best to make them work for you. Many people have found following these types of methods very helpful, but some may not have done – that's just life! A lot of it is dependent on how determined you are going to be. What works for one person, may not work for another person. Either way you must try your best and use this goal setting method - which is tried and tested - because writing down your goals is a very good way to start making things happen, and that's a fact! Once you have started achieving your goals you will then see how this method has worked for you and you will then be able to repeat the process each time you want to reach for another goal.

You should also enjoy the fact that you have reached one of your goals, revel in it, why not for goodness sake, haven't you worked hard and done the research in order to work your way up and get closer to your goal or dream step-by-step? So, when you have reached your goal, celebrate it and give yourself the credit you deserve for having achieved so much. At the end of the day, your future and your dreams and ambitions are in your own hands, this is something that not a lot of people realise, and for those who do; they write their lists and consistently take action, and they do so with purpose and the knowledge that they are the ones who have built it all up along the way. For those few who do follow this system and do these things, they will be the ones who will probably be reaching their goals, and if this is you right now, well done and welcome to the club.

"To show your true ability is always, in a sense, to surpass the limits of your ability, to go a little beyond them."
– Simone de Beauvoir

CHAPTER 27
Percentages

It may seem pretty unbelievable, but according to the research available at the time of this book going to press, most of the population does not set goals. Some people do set themselves goals, but they give up, and then other people do their goal setting, and they achieve their dreams – but these people are the ones who are in the minority!

Many people think about the goals and targets they would love to reach but are put off by the amount of work, time and effort needed to succeed. They think about it and realise that they don't even know where to begin, so instead they give up. Fear of change and stepping out of their box will also contribute to stopping them. Here are some of the statistics to help you to see how many people use this method of goal setting.

- 80% or more of new years resolutions are never completed.
- 80% of the population do not set any goals.
- 8% of people choose to go out there and do their tasks in order to reach their goals and succeed.
- 3% of people write down their goals and succeed in achieving them.
- 1% - yes, only 1% - of people review their goals each day and drive themselves forward to make their goals happen.

You can see from these statistics how very few people actually write their goals down and review them regularly and then go on to achieve their dreams. Most people do not organise themselves properly in order to be able to achieve results, or perhaps they choose to not take action out of the fear of failure. So, make a start and write your lists, and see how it can help you to succeed, give it a chance to succeed and be in the 3%, or even the 1%, of successful list makers and goal setters.

If you want to succeed you must get used to the fear of failure, in fact get used to the idea that you may well fail many times. This is nothing to be ashamed of, you could say that failures are a part of the journey to success. All of the successful people out there know this, and they will use any failures to their advantage; they choose to learn from it, they use these failures to drive them forward and failing actually makes them more determined to carry on. Sadly, as you can see from the statistics listed above, the majority of people don't do this and instead they give up because it is too hard; they don't know where to begin; they don't have a proper vision of a better future and maybe they can't be bothered to act because they lack the necessary drive and energy; maybe they have fears that mean they don't want to be laughed at, pointed out or even that they don't want to leave the safety of their box. It is okay if they want to live their lives that way – the tried and tested way – the known. Everyone has that choice, but hopefully you are reading this and thinking, 'I want more than this, I want to reach my goals.' Good for you! I'm not saying that the 80% can't change their minds and start goal setting, or that the 80% plus of those who failed to carry out their resolutions, cannot start again and achieve their goals this time around. If they want to then they can start again at any point and will hopefully decide to write down their goals, lists and tasks, in order to get better results should they decide to try again.

It can make a profound difference to how, or even if, a person will set goals if that person has grown up with parents who regularly set goals themselves. If a person did happen to have this experience growing up then this will put them at a distinct advantage to others, because it will seem like a normal part of life for them to set goals and go on to achieve them. So many people, however, do not have that experience as children and when they are growing up, as their parents didn't know about it, so goal setting will never have occurred to them and may actually seem like a strange concept. It will appear to them as though other people are just more successful, as if by magic or luck. It doesn't have to be that way. Don't let yourself be one of the 80% - the vast majority who do not set themselves any goals. Anyone can set goals for themselves and achieve them, especially if they make a habit of writing them down and following a plan. Most people just do not realise how easy it would be to reach their goals by using this method. They don't know about it and they are happy to continue as they are – just dreaming and not actually taking action in any way. I know that won't be you. You are the kind of person who wants more from life and wants to get things done, and I am sure you will.

Here is another statistic for you; 80% plus of people who had set new year's resolutions and goals, those people had given up by the middle of January! It has just proven too difficult for them to do. This is, of course, because they didn't write them down and work through their lists. All great self-development gurus have agreed that you should write down your goals to give yourself a much better chance of achieving them. In actual fact, I don't know of anyone who would disagree with this. Then there is the 8% or less who do actually set themselves goals, and who succeed, and it tends to be the case that those ones who did succeed were the ones who were breaking their goals down into bite size pieces – or steps – making it easier for them to achieve their goal. Reaching goals also has the added benefit of improving a person's psychological well-being each time that they meet a goal, and that 8% also reported an improvement in confidence and happiness levels if they completed a goal, which is not surprising.

The beauty of this goal setting technique is that anyone can do it, anytime and anywhere, and those who choose to do it this way always seem to have much better results by far. The more effort that you put into achieving your goals, the better your chance of success will be, of course, so start writing those lists and join the 3% club or even better the elite 1% club.

"Many of life's failures are people who did not realise how close they were to success when they gave up."
– Thomas Edison

CHAPTER 28
Acknowledge Your Progress

After completing your steps and reaching each of your goals you should acknowledge the progress you have made and give yourself a pat on the back. Well done!

I am sure that at every stage of your success and every milestone that you have passed, that you have shown gratitude and will have thanked anyone who may have helped you along the way. Gratitude is an important part of your journey, and so too is giving credit where credit is due to anyone who gave you advice or helped you out in some way. Of course, give yourself credit as well, not in a smug way but in that quiet and self-confident way that will find its way inside you and ignite an inner glow of contentment and happiness.

Even if you have not quite reached your goal yet, give yourself a pat on the back anyway, as you are still moving forwards in life toward success and taking the action that is necessary to gain whatever it is you are aiming for. Not everyone will buy a personal development book and take steps to change their lives. Many will just wish they were able to change things for the better and dream on without ever looking into how it can be done. Reading books like this one is a start and it will help you to succeed on your journey towards reaching a goal, of course, it is just one of the many things you could do to help yourself to get to where it is you are wishing to be, but it is still a pretty good start.

By reading this book you have shown that you want to change your life and achieve things, you have begun to take some actions, and that is a great thing to do. It shows ambition, determination and a willingness to start making improvements within your world. That sets you apart from so many other people who simply do not take any actions at all and instead just dream about the 'what ifs' and the 'if onlys'. Nothing changes unless you begin to take the right actions towards your goals – this book has, I hope, helped you to do just that, step by step. Well done! And now I will wish you good luck as you continue on with your goal setting, and your hopefully successful journey to achieving your goals and dreams.

"Be the change you want to see in the world."
– Mahatma Gandhi

Thank You Readers

Thank you for buying this book. I hope that it helps you achieve everything you want for yourself and more. I have faith that you can achieve a great deal in life when you put your mind to it. If this book helps only one person, then I will be happy to have helped in changing someone's life for the better, but I hope it helps a lot of people out there to get what they want and to reach their goals. Remember, never give up and never give in.

Good luck.

* If you are happy with this book, I would greatly appreciate it if you would leave a review on whatever platform you used to purchase this book*

Disclaimer

Although the author and the publisher have made every effort to ensure that the information in this book was correct at the time of going to press, the author and publisher do not assume and hereby disclaim any liability to any party for any loss, damage, injury or disruption caused by errors or omissions, whether such errors or omissions result from negligence, accident, or any other cause. This book is not intended as a substitute for the medical advice of physicians. The reader should regularly consult a physician in matters relating to his or her health and particularly with respect to any symptoms that may require diagnosis or medical attention. Reaching goals is fully the responsibility of the reader. The author and publisher do not guarantee any outcomes.

Acknowledgements

My parents, Dorothy and Peter Moffat. Thank you for everything you ever did for me. There isn't a day that goes by that I don't miss you both. God Bless you.

My partner, Graham Llewellin. Thanks for all your support and for always being there for me. Love you loads, you're a special guy.

Many thanks to all the experts and professionals who have helped me get this book published, in particular Val Hobbs for copy typing; Jessica Runyard for the editing and proof reading; and Tom Webb for formatting and the excellent cover design.

Many thanks to Mark Llewhellin for all your advice and mentoring which was invaluable. Mark is an author, marathon winner, interviewer of celebrities and many inspirational people. He is managing director of Mark 7 Productions and show host for the television series 'SAS – Who dares Wins' internet after show. Mark also hosts and produces speaking events around the UK.

Thanks must also go to all those friends who supported me and encouraged me in my book writing journey.

First published in Great Britain in 2021 by Angela Moffat

ISBN 978-1-5272-7975-9

Book design cover and formatting by Tom Webb.

www.ingramcontent.com/pod-product-compliance
Ingram Content Group UK Ltd.
Pitfield, Milton Keynes, MK11 3LW, UK
UKHW021631260325
5170UKWH00025B/288

9 781527 279759